NIPPLES OPTIONAL, A MEMOIR

An Ordinary Family with Unordinary DNA

Maureen Boesen
Kathryn Buckley
Bridget Stillwell
Paul Winn

Dedication

For the women who have nipples and to the women who don't,
Some of you will be given a choice and some of you won't.
For the women who use them and to the women who can't,
As well as those who choose to implant.
For the men and their non-functional nipples too...
but MOM,
This book is mostly for you.

CONTENTS

INTRODUCTION

We are three sisters who have taken drastic and controversial steps to alter our future. On top of the high risk of developing breast and ovarian cancer at a young age, we have battled infertility, anxiety, devastation, and loss. We are mothers, marathon runners, and advanced degree holders in business and science. Firsthand, we have experienced mastectomies, reconstructive surgery, and countless fertility treatments. Together we have faced obstacles in womanhood, motherhood, genetics-hood, and life in general.

It is our family's DNA that made us "famous." Our mother, Susan Winn, author of Chemo and Lunch, fought breast cancer at the age of 32 while raising four young children. She also fought to uncover an anomaly in our family history of breast and ovarian cancer dating back to the late 1800s. Her persistent fight helped lead to the identification of the BRCA1 mutation. This is not the claim to fame we hoped for in life.

Using DNA from our family, researchers were able to not only identify the BRCA1 mutation, but also confirm the validity of hereditary cancer, a concept that had been debated and disputed by the medical field for decades. This is the same BRCA1 gene mutation that celebrities Angelina Jolie and Christina Applegate inherited. These genuinely famous women helped make BRCA1 a household name, raising valuable awareness for genetic testing. Our goal is to raise awareness about the challenges of dealing with genetics and to discuss the importance of being an advocate for your own health including the pro gressive measures the three of us took to ensure our own good health and longevity.

Women talk about everything from changing hair color to changing jobs, changing clothes and, on occasion, changing husbands. Thanks to social media, we can instantly see when our friends get a new puppy or a big promotion. But what we do not discuss openly are our fears, our vulnerabilities, and how the medical decisions we make today affect the quality of our future. We share little about devastating miscarriages, follow-up mammograms, or preventive (prophylactic) double mastectomies. In addition, due to advancements in genetic testing, a glimpse into the future may reveal even more potential doom we may or may not want to address openly.

In this memoir, the three of us discuss our genetic and medical conditions and the resulting agonizing decisions with honesty and humor. What we've learned is that it's okay to share the not-so-pretty parts of life. The messy parts are the ones that connect us deeply to one another. We share our story for women of all ages who face these same complications or other new health dangers that threaten modern women today.

Too often women bear the weight of frightening health issues alone. In Nipples Optional, we encourage women to be open about their genetic dispositions, their futures, and their options. We invite you to join us and all the other strong, brave women around the world who have committed to become their own advocates.

PART I: BEFORE US

*Who is this ordinary family
with unordinary DNA?*

Dying Young

Before us, there were them. The women who came before us who carried a much heavier burden than we do. These
women are our ancestors, those with genetic targets on their
backs and a certain death sentence facing them. Before us, these
women were dying and they were dying young. They left behind large families and young children. Their deaths were inexplicable in nature, but all eerily similar.

One cold day in the 1960's, our grandmother, Elda, drove
to her cousin's house with a hot home-cooked meal to feed
seven suddenly motherless children. After the visit, our mother
who was a child at the time, heard our grandmother utter,
"There has been a lot of cancer in this family." Within four years
our mother would also be motherless. While our Grandmother
Elda recognized the rampant cancer in our family, she couldn't
prevent it from turning her into a victim. Our mother's mother
succumbed to cancer at just 44 years old.

For generations, our family had no knowledge of why so
many of its women, mothers to young children, were dying of
cancer. But what we sisters today are fortunate to know is who
these women were, why they died, and, in turn, why the three of
us are the way we are.

According to our mother, our great-grandmother, Grace,
(Elda's mother), was not a warm and fuzzy person. She never
hugged her granddaughter—our mother, Susan. And she was a
yeller. (An important note for our husbands: we inherited the
yelling/screaming gene from Great-Grandma Grace). Grace was
a hardworking farmer's wife and highly devoted to her Catholic
faith. As many good, practicing Catholics did at that time, she
went on to bear and deliver 10 children, who were all born at
home on the farm. The last one, Peter, did not make it. Family
members speculate that if he had been born in a hospital, he
would have survived.

Despite her grandmother Grace never hugging her, our
mother says she has fond memories of visiting her grandpar-

ents' farm. She especially loved strawberry picking. A picture of that family farm, where our mother spent years running around and skipping through cow manure with her 50+ cousins, still hangs in our parents' kitchen. While that picture provides our mom good memories, the reality is those years were clouded with the threat of cancer.

Our grandmother Elda was one of Grace and Phillip's 11 children. At the dinner table one evening, Elda, by then an adult, wife, and mother, cried as she told our mother that Grandma Grace was "sick." She could not bring herself to say the word cancer. Grace died at age 65 of ovarian cancer. Our mother was 11 years old. Although we have no documented proof of this diagnosis, our great grandmother very likely had the BRCA1 gene.

Shortly after the funeral, on Memorial Day in 1967, our mother and Elda visited Grace's grave. The fresh grave, plotted deep into the ground and surrounded by dewy, green grass, lay near other family sites. As our preadolescent mother explored the gravestones, she noticed the resting place of Grace's mother, Sophie, our mother's great-grandmother.

She knelt down to get a closer look at the headstone that read "Beloved Mother & Wife." In her head she did a quick calculation to determine her great-grandmother died at the mere age of 49, also from being "sick," our mother had been told. Her grandmother had just died at age 65 from being "sick." It dawned on our mother how young these women were, and even though her family didn't like to talk about it, everyone knew the women had died from cancer. That Memorial Day in 1967 is the first time our mother felt terrified by the word cancer. And rightfully so.

Three short years later, our grandmother Elda died. Our mother only had 14 brief years with her own mother. Her memories of her mother were that of a woman who was a hardworking, devout Catholic who liked to drink an occasional sherry or grasshopper on Christmas Eve, smoke, and dance. While her short and stocky stature only measured 5' 4", she was by no means a meek woman. Elda was one to fear. Behind her deep brown eyes and curly, thick hair (which the story goes could only be brushed by a sheep's brush), stood a woman with a temper—a temper that could be neutralized with a cigarette and nothing else. Elda had a softer side to her as well. She was said to always accept a late-night cuddle with her children and deeply loved her family.

As a child, our grandmother Elda attended a one-room schoolhouse where she was repeatedly slapped for using her left hand. Sadly, she never graduated from high school because she was needed on the farm to work. At the age of 19, Elda met and married our grandfather, Robert, shortly after he returned from World War II. After a short courtship, they secretly eloped. Elda and Robert were very much in love and started a family quickly, going on to have six living children, one being our mother.

Despite Elda's tough exterior and, at times, harsh parenting style, her death was extraordinarily traumatic for our mother. Before her death, Elda became increasingly more ill. Her abdomen became so bloated that women in the neighborhood speculated she was pregnant. Ironically, the cancer that took over Elda's body tortured her with pain for nine months.

In her dying days, Elda begged our mom, "Susie, just pray that I die," and that's exactly what our mother did. She prayed her own mother would die so she would no longer have to live in agony. In 1971, Elda, age 44, succumbed to some type of abdominal cancer, most likely believed to be ovarian. At just 14 years old, our mother watched her own mother suffer and die. Another woman in the family was dead, shaking our mother to her core.

This was a turning point in our mother's life. This is when she knew, without a shadow of a doubt, that something was wrong. She strongly suspected a familial component of cancer. Relatives were dying way too young, creating terror for everyone. And now her own mother had joined the list of the deceased. Who would be next?

Our mother believed she was destined to die of cancer at

a young age. So she decided she would have children before the age of 30. She was convinced that *when*, not *if*, she got cancer, it would happen in her 40s. Over the years, many doctors provided her assurance that cancer could not be hereditary, but this did little to calm her fears. The list of cancer victims in our family was too extensive to be a coincidence.

She lived in fear of cancer throughout her teen years, as a young bride, and as a mother to three daughters and a son. When our mother turned 30, after the birth of her fourth child, the ominous threat of developing cancer became very real to her. She decided to start researching the vast family tree to look for patterns of cancer and to determine if her fears were justified.

During her investigation, she connected with a distant cousin who kept excellent family records. Lois Sandusky was a cousin of our great-grandmother Grace. With Lois's help, our mother was able to piece together six generations and identify 650 descendants of our great-great-great grandparents, Joseph and Agnes Trunt. The common thread: early deaths.

Agnes Kanuith and Joseph Trunt were married in Poland and immigrated to the United States in the late 1860s. Their oldest son, Peter, died at the precious age of three just prior to their departure to America. They left his body behind to be buried by family because this was the last boat to the United States for many months. We speculate that on that boat from Poland to the United States, Agnes and Joseph carried more than their belongings. Agnes or Joseph likely carried within their DNA the BRCA1 gene mutation.

Joseph and Agnes came to the United States in search of a better life, freedom to own their own farmland and farm it as they please. It is important to note that Agnes did not die of cancer; she died in a farming accident at the age of 44. Agnes left behind Joseph and their 14 children.

One of the 14 children was Sophia Trunt Roskowyk, our maternal great-great-grandmother. Sophia was born in 1881 and died at age 49 of presumed colon, rectal, and stomach cancer. We now believe this was likely ovarian cancer that spread, but there were no reliable screening or diagnostic tools for ovarian cancer in the early 1900s.

Prior to her untimely death, Sophia and her husband John Roskowyk had five boys and one girl. Her only daughter was our great-grandmother Grace, who died of cancer in 1967.

Grace and Phillip produced ten children: two boys and eight girls, including our grandmother Elda Steffens Hare. Born in 1927, Elda, was the first of her ten siblings to die, at the age of 44, also of cancer. (Later, after testing became available, we learned seven of the ten siblings inherited the BRCA gene mutation.)

What our mother found in the family tree justified her reason to fear cancer. Her findings also made her determined to change her course of fate. Due to our mother's perseverance, extensive research, and hard work, she can be largely credited for uncovering the reason why so many women were dying prematurely in our family.

The Man, the Myth, the Geneticist

At the same time our mother was working to compile our family history, a geneticist in Nebraska was actively researching his theory of familial cancer. Dr. Henry Lynch of Creighton University School of Medicine was trying to prove that genetics played an important role in some cancer expressions.

While Dr. Lynch suspected cancer could be hereditary, the medical community did not support his suppositions. For 20 years, Dr. Lynch applied for research grants to allow him to study multiple generations of families with "cancer patterns." His requests for grants were denied year after year because experts did not believe cancer could be genetic.[iii]

Early theories of what caused cancer were vast. In the 1500s some experts believed cancer was contagious. Two doctors in Holland developed this theory when they observed breast cancers in the same household, i.e., familial breast cancers.[iv] In the 1960s and 1970s, modern theories about cancer arose. Many believed cancer was environmentally induced or perhaps caused by a virus.[v] During the time of Dr. Lynch's studies, some of these theories had long been debunked and others had been proven to be responsible for particular cancers, yet the idea that cancers could be inherited through DNA was still widely rejected. Many of Dr. Lynch's colleagues quite literally laughed at his theory that there could be a genetic link to cancer.

Dr. Lynch didn't pay much attention to the critics. He knew how to carve his own path. As a teen, he quit school at the age of 14. Two years later, he falsified his birth certificate so he could join the Navy at age 16. While in the Navy, he learned how to box and became a professional boxer (well-known as Hammerin' Hank) for a time.[vi] Eventually his path led him back to academics, where he developed a passion for genetics. Henry Lynch earned a PhD in Human Genetics and graduated from medical school at the University of Texas Medical Branch in 1960.

7

Dr. Lynch began as a resident in Internal Medicine at the University of Nebraska College of Medicine. There he cared for many cancer patients. Through these cancer patients' stories, he learned that some had high incidences of the same cancers existing throughout their family histories. These families sparked Dr. Lynch's curiosity in genetically fueled cancers, which became the focus of Dr. Lynch's work.[vii]

Through the coming years, Dr. Lynch worked tirelessly to prove his theories. He compiled lists of data from rural families' medical histories, leading him to identify cancer patterns throughout generations of extended families. In the early 1970s, Dr. Lynch's group at Creighton University provided some of the first evidence of an inherited trait that caused women to be predisposed to both breast and ovarian cancer, laying the groundwork for further studies.[viii]

Our mother learned of Dr. Lynch's research in 1988. She mailed him a letter with our family tree, highlighting the names of all the cancer victims. For her, it was a cry for help, and he answered.

Prior to any identification of the BRCA1 gene, our family became part of Dr. Lynch's campaign to identify hereditary cancer. Adults on our mother's side of the family, including cousins, aunts, uncles, donated blood and tissue samples to aid in the research conducted by the university and the Hereditary Cancer Institute. In collaboration with Dr. Steven Narod, a researcher from Canada, Dr. Lynch collected samples from each of our adult family members to see if the hereditary cancer secret could be unlocked. This work became known as Hereditary Breast/Ovarian Cancer syndrome, earning Dr. Henry Lynch the title "Father of Hereditary Cancer."[ix] And most importantly, the foundation of Dr. Lynch's research contributed to Dr. Mary-Claire King's discovery of the specific gene that threatened our family.

On March 28, 1992 (coincidentally, our grandmother's birthday, who had since passed away from cancer), Dr. Lynch's team traveled to Minneapolis to meet with our family, including nearby relatives, to share the results of his findings. The meeting took place in a hotel conference room off of Highway 494.

In the room sat Dr. Lynch, two of his staff members, our aunts (who remember the day as utterly emotional), and uncles with their respective spouses. The entire conversation only lasted 40 minutes.

Each family member was handed an envelope with their results of his research. Dr. Lynch went around the room and addressed each of our aunts and uncles individually. He presented their genetic results as fact.

Bear in mind, the BRCA gene mutation had yet to be formally discovered. Dr. Lynch was providing his hereditary cancer research findings. Yet there was no discussion of error rate or the possibility of there being any error at all. But also, no one doubted it or questioned it. Dr. Lynch explained that with a positive result, the chances of breast cancer were around 90% and ovarian cancer was around 60%. Our aunts recall receiving information on preventive surgery; however, Dr. Lynch held back making a formal recommendation.

What we didn't know then, we know now. Our family has a defective gene called the BRCA1 gene mutation. More accurately, we carry a defective *tumor suppressor* gene. You see, all humans carry BRCA genes. Our family's (and others' like ours) gene is slightly defected or mutated. It is mutated in a way that it does not suppress tumor development in cells as it should.

Dr. King identified this single gene mutation on chromosome 17q21 in 1994. She later named the mutation BRCA1.[x]

It is believed that seven of Grace and Phillip's ten children carried the BRCA1 gene. Five of the seven carriers were women. Only one of those five women lived to see past her 50s. We know for sure that three of the seven tested positive for the BRCA1 gene mutation. The other four died early in life but had children who tested positive for the mutation.

This potentially fatal BRCA1 gene has been passed down from generation to generation within our family. Agnes and Joseph immigrated from Poland most likely with the mutation in the 1860s. Their daughter, Sophia, passed it to her daughter, Grace. Grace passed it to her daughter, Elda, who passed it to our mother, Susan. Our mother passed it on to us. Well, some of us.

When our mother was young, she loved Doris Day. Every week, our mother would sit cross-legged on the worn-down, DuPont nylon carpet in front of the family's boxy square TV set. Captivated, she'd watch the beautiful, blonde actress sing her signature song, "Que Sera Sera," at the beginning of every show.

"Que Sera Sera
Whatever will be, will be
The future's not ours to see
Que Sera Sera"

Doris Day first sang "Que Sera Sera" in 1956, ironically the year our mother was born. Genetic testing did not exist in the mid-1950s. Medically, people believed that whatever will be, will be. There was no ability to see into the future. Back then, there was no way to prevent a hereditary cancer from stealing your life.

Genetic testing has changed that.

We are very fortunate because over the years great scientific strides have been made with genetic testing and improved treatment options for cancer. At the same time, there are skeptics who still don't believe in genetic testing. Some would disagree with the dramatic measures we have taken to alter our future.

But to us, "Que Sera Sera, Whatever will be, will be" seems absurd. The future *is* now ours to see.

Our mother fought to confirm her suspicion of a link to cancer in our family. Her determination helped us learn about the defective BRCA1 gene lurking within our family's DNA. Our mother gave us sisters an invaluable gift. She gave us knowledge —power—to save our lives.

We are the Winn sisters, and this is our story.

PART II: WHAT THE WINNS LOST

Dealing with low Las Vegas odds.

The Burden of Being First
Kathryn

I was the only girl in fifth grade who didn't wear a bra. My siblings and I attended the local Catholic grade school, where uniforms were mandatory. Thin, white uniform shirts do not look good on a fifth-grade girl just beginning to develop breasts. Surely my mother could see these tiny raisins underneath my shirt. Did she not think they looked as bad as I did? It took all the courage I could muster to ask my mom to buy me a bra. I agonized over it for weeks. With all of the attention around breasts in our family, you'd think talking about them wouldn't be a problem.

I wanted to explain to my younger sisters they had no idea what I was doing for them. They would never have to endure this humiliation since I was paving the way. However, they were only seven and nine years old at the time and not really at a point where I could explain the sacrifice of going first, much less the impending burden of puberty.

In addition to the bra request, I had some other burning questions for my mother that I figured I would ask while I had her attention. I wanted to start shaving the dark hair that was sprouting on my legs and easy to spot in those darn school uniform skirts. I also wondered what I was supposed to do when I got that dreaded monthly period all my girlfriends had begun to discuss.

I don't believe my mother intended for these uncomfortable issues to be so difficult for me to discuss with her. She was only 14 when she lost her own mother and I think she struggled with navigating these conversations. Maybe she handled growing pains on her own because she had no one to teach her. Or maybe back then these topics weren't discussed as openly as they are today.

I can hardly put the blame on my mom, though. I was a pre-teen navigating the tempestuous seas of adolescence. I didn't want to have these conversations any more than she did.

Especially since I was a typical firstborn and my main childhood goal was to please people and not cause any disruption. To the extent that on the rare occasion I snuck out in the middle of the night, I'd leave my parents a note—just in case they woke up and discovered I wasn't in my bed. The note would read: "I snuck out. Don't worry, I'll be careful. Be back by 4:00 a.m." I always sighed in relief when the note was exactly where I left it when I got home because I knew my parents never saw it.

I chose a crisp evening in late fall, my absolute favorite time of the year, to approach my mother with my questions. She sat alone on the couch in her robe and pink slippers, her regular evening attire (still to this day). In a ball of nerves, I whispered to myself, "Just do it." I had spent months rehearsing this crucial conversation.

My mom's feet were up, and she looked relaxed. I sat down next to her, probably a little too close because I was so anxious. The conversation lasted less than two minutes.

"Mom, I need to talk to you about a few things."

"Okay."

"I need a bra."

"Why?"

"Because all my friends have one." (Oddly enough, that wasn't even the real reason. It was because you could see my nipples.)

"Okay, I'll get you a training bra."

This was not the response I wanted. I wanted her to take me shopping for a cute, little pink bra with bows like my friends were wearing.

The next topic went a bit easier. She told me I could start shaving but it would be something I would always have to do once I started. At the time, I didn't understand what my mother meant, nor did I care. Just get me a razor.

The period conversation ended our talk.

"*When* you get your period, let me know and I'll buy you some pads. If it happens when I'm not home, my pads are under my bathroom sink."

The next day, I walked into my bedroom after school, and on my bed I found a razor alongside a thin, little piece of string that basically resembled a bra but could hardly be called a bra. I sat down on my hunter green carpet with my back up against my daybed and held the tiny string between my fingers, relieved this conversation was over, yet disappointed in the outcome. This so-called "bra" only accentuated my nipples under that thin, white uniform shirt. I still don't look good in thin white shirts no matter how many padded pink bras I can buy myself.

Luckily, my period didn't show up for a few more years. And when it did, I wasn't happy.

"This isn't fair. Why do I have to have a period? I don't even want children," I grumbled as I sat on the toilet scouring over the Tampax directions on how to insert a tampon.

If I had only known the universe was actually listening to me when I said that, I would have never uttered those stupid words.

When I was a senior in high school, my face broke out in flat warts. Small, brown circular flat warts erupted on my face, around my mouth, and up through my cheekbones. Standing in the Jack and Jill bathroom that separated my room from my sister's room, I would lean over the sink, stare at my face, and cry. Warm tears stung as the tears flowed over my wart-infested face. I tried everything to get them to go away. Numerous medications made my face dry out, crack, and bleed. I even tried toothpaste at one point. I was desperate.

As a teenage girl about to go to prom and eventually college, I was mortified. I felt as though everyone was staring at me. I couldn't hold a conversation or look anyone in the eye because I was sure they were thinking my face was hideous. (Little did I know, I would have the exact same feeling at age 35, but from a completely different issue.)

On one particular bad flat wart face day, my mother came up to my room. She sat at the edge of my bed and looked at me with understanding in her eyes.

"If you don't want to go to school today, you don't have

to."

My mom gave me permission to stay home from school because she understood my embarrassment.

At that moment, I looked at her with tears in my eyes, tied my white, Converse All Stars and went to school. I couldn't stay home long enough for the warts to disappear. Those damn flat warts lasted all the way through the middle of my freshman year in college, until one day I woke up and they were gone. They literally just vanished.

I still have major fears the ugly warts will reappear some-day. I Google flat warts about once a year at the slightest sign of a small, brown raised spot on my face. Usually the internet tells me I have a new freckle or worse, a mole. On rare occasions, the internet suggests I might have flat warts again.

Could these flat warts have been inherited? Chances are unlikely since flat warts are a virus.[xi] But do my genes play a role into why I had flat warts? Quite possibly yes. What lies within our DNA makes us more susceptible to certain viruses over others.

As far as I know, I did not inherit flat warts from my mother, but I did inherit a lot from her. I have her exact dirty dishwater, brown hair and light brown skin and medium brown eyes. I was lucky enough to inherit her overly crooked toes, for which she has had three surgeries to straighten. I see toe surgery in my future. I also like to think I inherited her strength and per-severance, which I did not realize until later on in life.

What I did not inherit from my mother was the very thing that put my family on the map—the BRCA1 gene mutation.

Classic
Bridget

I was just three years old when my little sister, Maureen, was born. There I was—smack in the middle of two girls and one boy. Kathryn, my big sister, fills the role of quintessential oldest child and matriarch—always has and always will, I expect. She's truly the best older sister anyone could ask for. My brother, Paul, came right on the heels of Kathryn, just one and a half years later. Then came me, not even two years after Paul. Maureen didn't come until I was three years old, but needless to say, things were busy in our home.

I can be described as a classic middle child, and that is exactly what I was as a kid—an attention-seeking story embellisher. I wasn't the oldest, I wasn't the youngest, and I wasn't the only. My parents never treated me any differently than any of my siblings, though I just couldn't help but feel like I didn't have a place.

What is so special about me? I often wondered.

I didn't know things were going to get a lot harder in my life than simply where I randomly landed in the birth order in my family. And none of us could have predicted the shocking course of events that, in the end, set me apart from my two sisters.

My mother always said her years of raising young children were the best years of her life. I find this really beautiful and also a little odd. While she was raising four young children, she was also fighting for her life against breast cancer. By the time our mom received her diagnosis, the cancer had already spread.

She believed there was a good chance she was going to die and had even picked out her casket dress and a new wife for my dad. She told my father he needed to remarry quickly because she did not want the burden of raising siblings to fall on my older sister, Kathryn. My mother isn't afraid to tell it like it is with little emotion to spare.

As children, we never felt the stress my parents were

under or the impact of her illness. I don't think I ever even sensed anything was amiss. This is an extraordinary feat considering that if I even have the slightest headache, my children better make themselves scarce.

I had a lovely childhood. We were a typical suburban family living in a decent-sized suburban home. A large u-shaped couch—the center point of our 1980s inspired home—faced our extremely large television. Framed in light oak wood and weighing about 500 pounds, our first "big screened TV" was my father's pride and joy. As a successful pharmaceutical salesman, he had won the TV as an award for being one of the top salesmen in the region. My first memory of this enormous television was watching TGIF (Thank Goodness It's Friday) on Friday night in our footed pajamas with a large, orange bowl of popcorn. My second memory of the TV is my mom yelling at my dad every time we moved, "I am never moving that F&%@$*# television again!" A large, brass lamp hung over the middle section of the couch and top-to-bottom bookshelves lined the wall, holding our massive Encyclopedia Britannica and family pictures. At one point a gerbil cage sat on the shelves but that was about as short lived as the gerbil.

We lived on a cul-de-sac littered with children and young families, with a swing set in our backyard where the neighborhood kids often played together.

My mother drove a maroon minivan with faux wood siding. This van had a personalized license plate that said, "Winivan." My parents were so proud of their humorous and creative license plate, our last name being Winn and all. The van was even wrapped with gray pinstriping and within the stripes "Winivan" was written in cursive. I can't make this stuff up. My parents later sold this van to a man with one leg. This detail is not at all important to my story, but a fitting fate of the Winivan with faux wood siding and a family's name inscribed in the pinstriping.

My parents loved holidays and worked hard to make each holiday distinctly special. One year they even had a real bunny hopping around the house on Easter Morning. "The Easter Bunny stayed!!!" the four of us siblings shrieked.

My parents are remarkable people. They were raised with very little money and worked for everything they got. They both obtained higher education, despite minimal support from their families, and became successful in their careers. Yet they are self-described cheap people and made sure to instill a good work ethic in their children.

When I turned 14, my parents demanded I get a job. There were limited job opportunities for kids at that age, but sacking groceries was one of the few. Sacking groceries for neighbors and friends was utterly humiliating, but it was important to my parents that we knew the value of working hard no matter who you are. So with a broach on my collar, a smile on my face and swear words in my head, I swallowed my 14 year-old tween pride and I sacked groceries. My parents weren't afraid to show us that, in life, the harder you work the better life will be.

It turns out I am eternally grateful for the work ethic our parents instilled in me, along with the ability to swallow my pride. This was something I would repeatedly need to do in the future many times over.

My Mother's Baby
Maureen

I was two years old when my mother was diagnosed with breast cancer. From what I am told, I called my mother's breasts "owies" because, to a two-year-old, that's exactly what they were. My mother was recovering from chemotherapy and a double mastectomy but, to me, all I could see were boo-boos. I'm sure someone sat my siblings and me down at one point and told us our mom had cancer, but I certainly don't remember it.

A woman we dubbed "Grandma Dorothy" came to our house to watch us while my mother drove herself to chemo once a week. At the time, I didn't know why Grandma Dorothy was there. She may have looked like a grandma, but she wasn't *our* grandma. My mother claims Grandma Dorothy just showed up on our doorstep one day, like an answer to her prayers. Since my mom was convinced Dorothy was an actual angel, she didn't think twice about leaving her four small children with a perfect stranger.

What I also remember about my mother's breast cancer diagnosis was her being very sad. How could she not be, after all? This disease had stolen her mother's life and her grandmother's life. Was it going to steal hers, too?

One afternoon I walked down the hallway and into her bathroom. My mother was sitting on the carpeted bathroom floor, crying. I don't know if I saw the brush she was holding or maybe the hair that lay in her hands, but I knew her hair had begun to fall out. I sat next to my mother and hugged her. She was very sad, and even at the age of two, I understood. Is it possible to create your first memory at the age of two? Most experts would say it is doubtful. Unless, of course, it is a memory as profound and significant as this one. My mother remembers that day too, although until recently she had never told me.

I'm thankful my mother didn't die from breast cancer. However, if she had, we would have had a spare.

Enter me.

From our chicken legs to our borderline ADD to our endless creativity, I am she and she is me. In many uncanny and particular ways, my mother and I are the same.

We were born without filters on our mouths, which is unfortunate because we both happen to have the mouth of a sailor.

We are ambitious, we are witty, and we are not morning people.

We love to run long distances, yet our stride is very, very short.

No one can tell us no. Try, I dare you.

We are independent and spontaneous.

Halloween is life for us and there is no birthday cake too difficult to decorate.

I am my mother's baby and I secretly adored it when she would often refer to me as just that, her baby. Even as a teenager, she would still tell other mothers that I was her baby, in reference to me being her youngest. I wore that as a badge of honor (I still do, to be honest).

I am her fourth born and, incidentally, my mother is also a fourth born.

We have more in common than not.

As a child, I used to wonder when I would get breast cancer, like my mom. To me, it wasn't a matter of if, but when. I didn't really worry about getting cancer, and I certainly didn't worry about dying from cancer. If my mom could get it and beat it, so could I. Plus, there would be a cure for cancer by the time I'm that age, I told myself.

As it turns out, breast cancer wasn't my cross to bear like it was my mother's.

Not Out of the Woods Yet
Kathryn

In the late 1980s, a decade of lace drapes and light-colored wood, our do-it-yourself mother (she was DIY before DIY was cool) hung white textured wallpaper throughout our dining room and accessorized with multiple shades of hunter green and maroon. The glossy lacquered dining table served as the room's main attraction, but its purpose extended way beyond food.

The large oval table was reserved for special meals, specifically the "Winn Cafe." Our parents did an annual breakfast for us where we could order whatever we wanted from the menu they created. And, as a child with three siblings, getting whatever I wanted was a rarity. (Our parents still do the "Winn Cafe" for their grandchildren, although they have upgraded their dining room table to some fancy table that includes a set of chairs that cost more than my first car.)

But most of the time during our childhood, our mother stood over our dining room table, papers scattered end-to-end, as she endeavored to map out the entire family history of breast and ovarian cancer.

She had been gathering as much family history as possible. Packages arrived in the mail (the internet and email did not exist yet) to open and pour over. She documented pictures and names and health details, writing the word "deceased" on the relatives' names who were no longer with us, citing the cause of death and making extra notes near the cancer victims' names.

Our mother's father was a calculating man with white, wavy hair that swooped across his forehead, giving him a distinguished yet gentle-hearted look. He observed the extreme effort our mom devoted to her mission. One day when our grandfather came to visit, he saw Mom laboring at the dining table, opening mail and taking more notes, and he made a comment that lit a spark in our mother.

"Susie, you are never going to change the world!"

I believe this is the exact statement that sparked a fierce fire inside her—a fire that would ultimately change our lives and arguably the world.

Ironically enough, our mother became a breast cancer victim in the midst of her extensive research. In 1988, our mother was diagnosed with stage II breast cancer at age 32. She was sad and scared, but not surprised.

She was also very angry. Our mother had always planned to have preventive surgery at the age of 30 but was talked out of it by her physician who thought she was crazy. What no one knew at the time she was studying the family tree to determine a link between genetics and breast cancer, her own genetically fueled cancer was already growing inside her body.

Our mother had bilateral mastectomies, seven months of weekly chemotherapy, and a total hysterectomy. My siblings and I were ages eight, seven, five, and two at the time of her diagnosis.

While our mother was going through chemotherapy, Dr. Lynch was still working to uncover the mystery of why so many women had fallen to cancer in our family. After many conversations with our mother about his research, he requested we come for further research.

This time, he wanted to study blood samples from my siblings and me to search for a pattern within our bloodwork. Our parents didn't need to discuss. It was quite simple—they wanted answers. They did not want to watch any of us go through what our mother was currently going through.

My siblings and I were much too young to understand the importance of what we were doing, but our mom knew.

She told the nurse who drew our blood that day, "This is history in the making!"

The nurse looked at our mom like she had four heads, but our mom knew what she was talking about. The researchers studied our samples and recorded the results—results the researchers would not allow us to see until we each reached the age of 18.

Five years later, in 1994, we received a letter from Dr. Lynch. Our cancer-riddled ancestors were no longer a mystery. The BRCA1 gene mutation had been discovered.

The hypothetical gene was real. It had a location. It had a name.

This autosomal dominant gene means a person with it has a 50/50 chance of passing it to an offspring. This BRCA1 gene had caused so many premature deaths of our ancestors. Now a blood test could determine if someone inherited the gene.

Thankfully, although our mother carried the BRCA1 gene, she survived breast cancer and was able to raise her four children and nine grandchildren. Later on in life she shared with us how frightened she was of our (my siblings and myself) future. The fate of our future had been decided long ago and it was fast approaching for each of us.

In 2001, at the age of 21, I decided to learn my fate. I wanted to know if I had inherited this mutation that had plagued so many of the women before us. I could have found out the results as early as age 18. My parents, who were very supportive, did not pressure me, but let me decide when I wanted to receive the results. Interestingly, I did not feel stressed or worried about the results. One day I simply said to my parents, "It's bothering me more not to know than to know." So, we made the journey together to meet with Dr. Lynch.

My parents and I sat with Dr. Lynch and a genetic counselor around a large meeting table in the Hereditary Cancer Institute at Creighton University in Omaha. The room looked like it could belong on the 56th floor of a Fortune 500 company yet smelled like a hospital. We sat in oversized chairs that couldn't decide if they wanted to be an office chair or a recliner. I started to feel uncomfortable as Dr. Lynch and the counselor took turns discussing the testing and potential results with us.

My eyes stayed on the envelope in Dr. Lynch's hands. It contained not only my future but also my siblings' futures. How my mother did not jump across the table and rip the folder out of his hands, I'll never know.

Dr. Lynch slowly opened the folder, my body went numb, and my hands began to sweat.

I watched Dr. Lynch's eyes as he read the report of my results. It didn't take long for him to look up, take off his glasses, and look straight into my eyes. He spoke very slowly and deliberately.

"You are *not* a carrier of the BRCA1 mutation."

I felt relieved, but not happy. I sensed the same feeling from my parents.

Dr. Lynch presented this great news in a glum sort of way. Before we left, he said, "Your family is not out of the woods yet." Dr. Lynch knew the results of my remaining three siblings.

As we drove back to Kansas City, I sat silent in the back of my parents' tiny, black 2001 BMW. In my head, I replayed the conversation with the genetic counselor about the odds of having the gene. If I didn't have the BRCA1 gene, that meant some of my other siblings most likely *did* have it. I couldn't bear to watch any of my siblings suffer or go through something that might potentially take them from me.

Clearly, this is why my parents were not happy. They, too, realized that if it was not me who had the gene mutation, then who was it going to be? This was our first Winn family experience with genetic testing; we did not realize the impact this knowledge would have on us.

For me, more genetic testing lay ahead in my future—for a completely different reason.

Bridget the Midget
Bridget

As picturesque of a childhood as I experienced, trauma began early. At the same time my parents were trudging through my mother's cancer diagnosis, I was quickly falling behind in school. My parents, as well as teachers, noticed I was struggling, but no one wanted to pull the trigger until they had no choice. By the third grade, it became abundantly clear that I couldn't keep up with even the simplest of curriculum. The decision was eventually made that I couldn't move ahead and must repeat third grade.

Was I learning disabled? No.

Was I undiagnosed/unmedicated ADD? Sure.

I believe I slipped through the cracks until third grade likely due to the crisis at home and teachers who were too sweet to say anything about stupid little Bridget because her mom had cancer and things were already shitty enough for the Winn family.

Fortunately for me, my family moved away from Kansas the year my parents decided to hold me back, so none of my classmates or friends knew. For the next four years, we moved around to several states due to my father's pharmaceutical sales profession. It probably helped that I was physically short, which consequently earned me the nickname "Bridget the Midget," and I blended in fine with the other students who were a year younger than me.

I especially loved grades four and five in Pennsylvania. I suppose you could say I was popular. A boy even wanted to kiss me on my last day of school. I was disgusted at the thought of kissing a boy in fifth grade and immediately declined. I can still remember him very well. Jason Scott Layton and his favorite color was purple. He had thick, wavy brown hair and he wore circle glasses. Maybe I should have kissed him after all. Oh well.

Eventually, our dad's job led us back to Kansas City—the place all six of us really thought of as "Home Sweet Home." Moving back to KC was thrilling for all of us. It would be our final move as a family.

It didn't occur to me that I would run into my old classmates... until I did. I ended up at the same Catholic grade school for my middle school years that I had left four years prior. I was in sixth grade and, of course, my old friends were in seventh grade. I somehow thought, *hoped,* maybe they wouldn't notice me or remember me. No such luck. On my very first day back a girl named Caroline pointed at me in front of everyone and screamed, "BRIDGET WINN IS IN SIXTH GRADE!!!"

I was mortified.

My stupid past followed stupid me, Bridget the Midget, and it would continue to follow for many years to come.

For as long as I can remember, I had an internal debate about when I wouldn't feel so stupid anymore. Would I ever be able to escape the humiliation of being held back, being stupid, not being good enough? I was deeply ashamed of myself. These feelings were painfully embedded in me and, for a young girl, they were difficult to sort out. I needed someone to help me understand what had happened. I needed someone to tell me that I was not, in fact, stupid, but I learned differently than other kids. I needed someone to tell me that I was good enough. As best I can remember, I was never told. And it took its toll on me.

I acted out. I lied. I stole. I snuck around. I hated myself. But I was smart enough to realize that I couldn't last like that.

Eventually I learned, then mastered, the skill of positive self talk. This became my life line to prevent me from crumbling under the pressures of life. Motivational conversations with myself would play on repeat in my head until I began to believe in myself. Positive self talk was a priceless trait that evolved from a little girl who was very lost and needed to find her way. This is a trait that I have used in every challenging circumstance life has thrown my way. Creating a resilient attitude was not only important, it was necessary because being held back as a young child was just the beginning of my bumpy road ahead.

I was too young to remember my mother enduring cancer and chemotherapy, but it was always something we talked about. In fact, my first vivid memory was the day my blood was drawn to test for a gene that hadn't been identified yet. Over the years, my parents and I never had one particular conversation about the possibility of me being a BRCA1 mutation carrier. It just seemed to be understood. Somehow, I always knew I was going to be a carrier. I was positive that I was "positive."

Due to stipulations of the research study, participants could not be informed of their genetic results until the age of 18. The reasoning for this is that there is nothing a person can do prior to that age and the researchers worried about the psychological implications if the results are revealed to an individual too soon. I chose to wait until I was 21 to find out my genetic status. I knew it was time because I would find myself lying awake in bed at night mulling over my genetic status.

My gynecologist connected me with a local genetic counselor, Amy, who had an office just up the street at a local hospital, Menorah Medical Center. That hospital would later be home to some of the most defining moments of my life, including major surgeries and beautiful babies. This hospital was one of the newest hospitals in our area and had a far from hospital feel. Fresh plants and waterfalls filled the open spaces. Just across the hall from Amy's office was an outdoor oasis. I always wondered who ever sits out there.

My mother, father, and I sat across from Amy one Friday morning in May of 2004 to discover my genetic status. On the desk in front of us, I saw an unopened manila folder with my name on it. My future, maybe my death sentence, lay right there at Amy's fingertips.

A box of Kleenex also sat on her desk. I was very focused on that box of Kleenex. *Will I need to use that Kleenex to dry my tears when she tells me I'm positive?* I wondered.

The four of us engaged in some small talk. Then she asked an odd question.

"Bridget, do you have life insurance?"

"No."

I was only 21. Of course I didn't have life insurance.

Amy took a deep breath, and then continued, "Before I open this folder, I think it would be a good idea for you to do that."

With her statement, but without an official result, I knew I was positive. I carried the BRCA1 gene mutation.

A Promise to Myself
Maureen

The process to discover whether I carried the BRCA1 gene mutation began in the midst of my mother's battle with breast cancer. At the age of three, I sat with my mother and siblings in a doctor's office, waiting to have my blood drawn and tested for the gene mutation.

"Maureen, you're up."

I slowly walked toward the nurse and followed her back to the clinical room. She had me climb up onto the table, lie down, and turn my head away from the needle. I lay there staring at a wall covered in balloons or clowns of some sort as she began to draw blood out of my left arm. The blood she was drawing would predict if I, like my mother, would develop breast cancer.

However, it would be another 17 years until I learned the results of that test.

It is without coincidence that I pursued my undergraduate degree at Creighton University—the same university that conducted the research my family participated in nearly two decades prior. My family held the university in very high regard. And why would we not? Dr. Lynch had given my family insight to our DNA well before it was known or commercially available. We felt indebted to him. We were thankful for him.

So, when I began looking at universities to attend, I wasn't surprised when my father suggested, "Let's look at Creighton. I think you'll like Omaha."

My father was right. (Insert eye roll.) I had an incredible experience at Creighton. And, oddly enough, I fell in love with Omaha. (I also fell in love with a boy. He was so much of what I pictured for myself—a brown haired, Catholic, Creighton grad who was two years older than me—that I couldn't let him go.) What I loved most about Creighton was its greater purpose. The university was so much more than a school where I spent four years studying, partying, and meeting some of the greatest people—Creighton University was committed to research, saving lives, and making a difference in this world.

Incidentally, two buildings beyond where I studied marketing, was the Hixon Lied science building—the building where researchers and doctors had studied my blood 17 years earlier as part of the discovery of the BRCA1 gene mutation.

As a university student I didn't find myself in the Hixon Lied science building very often. I did wander in there a time or two looking for an attractive male medical student to "help a lost business student find her way," although, for the most part, I stayed as far away as I could from any college course related to science. This is further evidenced by my required science credit being completed with Astronomy 101.

However, on Friday, June 6, 2008, I sat in the middle of Hixon Lied to learn my genetic results. The time had come for me to find out just exactly how much my mother and I had in common.

To be honest, I wasn't in a rush to find out. Of course, I wanted to know my results, but I had been perfectly content waiting. At the time, I didn't know what I had been waiting for. But it became clear to me that I was waiting for Bridget to go first. I needed my older sister to show me the way.

I can't remember a time when I didn't look up to Bridget and look for her guidance in life. In my eyes, Bridget and I are more alike than not. I have always thought Bridget and I look the most similar out of the Winn siblings, but I think that has more to do with our mannerisms than our facial features. Bridget and I also often think very similarly. She just gets me, on maybe a level that others never will. I attribute this to having nearly identical DNA. I have a connection with her that I can only compare to what I imagine the connection is between twins. I can talk to Bridget several times a day on the phone and spend the majority of the time laughing hysterically. If we aren't laughing, we are solving the world's problems. And when it came to solving our genetic problems, Bridget, in true Bridget fashion, showed me the way.

Bridget navigated her BRCA1 gene mutation inheritance with strength and grace. I watched from afar and prayed I could do the same.

I was about to be a senior in college and near the end of my time at Creighton. I knew what needed to be done. I thought to myself, *I guess it's my turn.* So I called the Creighton Heredity Cancer Center and scheduled my appointment.

I had pictured this meeting in my mind for a very, very long time, most likely since I learned about Kathryn's results. That day many years earlier, my parents had picked me up from a month away at summer camp and as soon as I got in the car, they told me Kathryn was negative. I felt no relief at all when I heard the news. *The mutation is in someone's DNA,* I thought to myself, *but whose?* We later learned Bridget was positive. Would I be positive too?

So, there I sat with my mom, dad, and Bridget, waiting anxiously in Hixon Lied 202. A woman from the Department of Preventive Medicine asked me a series of questions that she said in no way indicated whether or not I had the gene.

"When did you find out about the BRCA gene?"

I told her I can't remember a time when I didn't know. She said that was common with families who have actually *had* cancer but living with the knowledge of having the BRCA gene is more difficult with families who *don't* develop the cancer. I found that ironic. I wondered what I would tell my children someday. *Would not developing cancer make this harder or easier?*

"From 1 to 100, what do you think your chances are of inheriting the gene, knowing that the chances are 50%?" she asked.

I said 75%, although I actually thought it was more like 99%. I told her I've grown up knowing the possibilities and being prepared for the possible outcomes. What I didn't tell her was that the gene was a part of who I was, whether I inherited it or not.

After she asked me a series of other questions, she left to get Dr. Lynch. As soon as the nurse was gone, my mom said, "I think you have the gene." That's my mom for you. One thing I already knew I inherited from my mom was her bluntness.

Dr. Lynch came in after about ten minutes and, initially, I was unattracted to his demeanor. I was thankful for his research and I think he was a brilliant man, however, as he leaned back in his chair with his disheveled grey hair, he seemed distant from our conversation, a conversation that was about to change my life.

We discussed his research of hereditary breast cancer and the contributions he made to the genetics community with the findings from our samples. He said he wanted to get a better idea of what I was thinking and asked if I had any questions.

I thought for a moment then asked, "Is there any chance the results could be wrong?"

While I trusted him, a little voice in my head had to ask. As the words came out of my mouth, I pictured vials and vials of blood in his lab all labeled with different names and results. The ease at which one could get switched felt apparent to me.

"It's just not possible," he declared.

The conversation continued with my parents asking questions and Dr. Lynch giving answers.

At one point, Dr. Lynch commented, "I wouldn't go to Vegas with your odds, or you'll be riding home in a bus."

The nurse and Dr. Lynch did a good job of appearing neutral while knowing my results, although low Vegas odds revealed a pretty obvious sign of my destiny. The conversation went on for a while after that.

Why would we still be talking about this if I was negative?

In the middle of the conversation, Dr. Lynch stopped abruptly and announced, "You inherited the mutation." The rest of the conversation was a blur.

After our parents left, Bridget and I returned to my college house to find Alisha, my roommate, who was anxiously waiting for answers. If anyone understood, it was Alisha. She was not only supportive; she genuinely cared. Maybe it was because her aunt died from breast cancer. Maybe it was because we understood each other. We had been through a lot together and I was fortunate to have her to go through this with me.

Standing in the entryway of our house, I told her the results.

She hugged me for a long time and finally said, "You are acting shockingly cavalier."

I took it as a compliment, although I'm pretty sure it is a quote from the movie *Juno*.

I called Josh, my then boyfriend and now husband, to tell him the news. I think he expected what I was about to tell him. He is very much a realist, which is a blessing and a curse. Josh is the only person who didn't reply by saying, "I'm sorry." I appreciated that. There was nothing to be sorry about. These were the cards we were dealt.

Josh understands, too. Having to live with a chronic disease (Crohn's), he knows you deal with it and move on. What is the point in dwelling on it? Instead, we must choose to do something about it.

Bridget and I climbed into my 2002 Silver Honda Civic and made the three-hour drive to Kansas City. On the way, I called my brother, Paul, to let him know my results.

Paul attempted to comfort me by saying, "You know I have the gene, too."

I still chuckle to myself when I think about him saying this. In no way did it comfort me at the time. He didn't have to have his breasts chopped off. But, at the same time, what he was really saying to me is that we were family, and we were in this together. And that was the most comforting thing anyone could have said.

What I learned that day is that it's impossibly hard to hear the news you have a gene that could steal your life. I imagine it's a million times harder to hear you have a cancer that *is* stealing your life. I promised to not let that happen.

PART III: BAD GENES OR BAD LUCK?

*Or perhaps a bad
combination of both?*

Extended Vacation
Kathryn

After learning my genetic test results in the summer of 2001, I wrapped up my blissful, worry-free college years—and I say worry-free because I didn't worry very much about the future once I learned I did not carry the BRCA gene. In hindsight, I *should* have worried a little more in college and taken it slightly more seriously. I had just assumed I would get a degree, get a job, get a husband, and move through my life with ease. And, I did, for a while.

Shortly before graduating, I met my tall, handsome, future husband. And for some inexplicable reason he found me attractive, although I question his sense of judgment. I was still stuck in the 90s with a hairstyle that can only be described as a mix between "the Rachel" and "Princess Diana." My fashion style consisted mostly of turtlenecks (because I thought they made me look sophisticated) and overalls that I purchased from Gap Kids. I didn't have money to spend on designer clothes like my friends did with their new big paychecks.

The title of my first job was Associate Financial Advisor, which really meant glorified secretary to a Financial Advisor. My duties included paperwork, filing, making copies and more filing. My first salary matched my responsibilities: little to none. I made just enough to put gas in my car but not enough to move out of my parents' house or buy expensive things. This was mostly due to my lack of worry about college and my future.

Nonetheless, Bryan Buckley married me and my credit card debt in May 2004. Bryan is a very motivated, and motivating person. Whatever he puts his mind to, he accomplishes. I jumped on that train with him, landed myself a fantastic career, and worked my way up the ranks to a Vice President role while earning my MBA. We decided together we would enjoy being DINKs (dual income, no kids) for a few years and then add to our family later. As if it were just that easy.

In February 2007, we decided it was time to create some little Buckleys. What better way to start this adventure than kicking it off in Maui on a "procreation vacation?" As we boarded that 737 bound for paradise, I was much more excited than Bryan. He would have been content staying in the comfort of our own bedroom.

"Why the heck do we have to go all the way to Hawaii to start a family?"

Our trip began with a delayed flight, a missed connection, and a seven-hour layover in Dallas. This foreshadowed our future well. It would be seven long years before we added any Buckleys to this family.

During our seven-hour layover, Bryan and I wandered around the bustling Dallas airport buying random crap we didn't need from stores we didn't recognize. I picked up an expensive book on tape, a purchase Bryan deemed unnecessary and said so. I was in this fight now. *Who is my husband to tell me what I need or do not need for my Hawaiian procreation vacation?*

"I will use this all the time," I mumbled as I paid for the book on tape that I never actually got around to listening to. In the back of my head, I wondered, *Will I have to run all decisions by my husband from now on?*

This thought turned into a reality as soon as we left the Duty-Free shop.

"I want five children, all close in age," I casually remarked as we joined the rest of the hurried travelers making their way through the airport.

"You do?!"

"How do you not know this?" I threw back at him without leaving him time to respond. "I plan on staying at home and taking care of our children, so wouldn't I be the one who has more say in how many children we have?"

"Babe, I just have never wanted five children," he said lovingly. "It seems so busy and so expensive. Plus, the more children, the more problems."

"I hate to burst your picturesque bubble, but we could

have one child and he or she could be a problem. Why do you liken multiple children to problems?"

To this question, he did not have an answer. Bryan grew up with only one brother. I grew up in a lively household with children bouncing around, lots of activities to get to, abundant laughing, and loud voices. I expected to have the same kind of family with my husband. And I wanted to be as involved and present of a mother as mine was to me.

I didn't realize until much later in life how hard my parents worked. My mom ran us all over the city and had dinner on the table each night, all while fighting cancer.

It was dark by the time we arrived at our hotel in Maui. Exhausted from the day, and quite frankly from the conversation about children, we went directly to our room and went to bed. We did not have the energy to look around our beautiful hotel or even eat dinner. However, when we woke up the next morning, we felt like we'd been transported into a fairy tale.

"Look out the window. This is the most beautiful thing I have ever seen!" Bryan exclaimed.

Our room overlooked the clear blue ocean. The palm trees and beach stretched on for miles, and there was not a cloud in the sky as the smell of ocean air drifted into our room. *Our procreation vacation has begun!*

Our procreation vacation to Maui turned into a procreation vacation to Mexico, and one to California, and one to Florida. Turns out, my perfect plan of getting pregnant did not work out the way I had planned. It never once occurred to me I would have trouble getting pregnant. Every single month for two years I believed I would get pregnant, but every single month for two years, I did not get pregnant. After two exhausting years, I finally admitted to myself that just maybe we had a problem.

This wasn't part of my plan. We were supposed to have babies! Lots and lots of babies! I wanted to pretend infertility wasn't happening to us, but after trying for so long I couldn't hide anymore. We needed help.

I slowly opened up to some of our closest loved ones that

we were having trouble. When I shared with my mother, her response took my breath away and boiled my blood at the same time.

"You don't want to be 40 and childless, wishing you would have done something," she said, "This [fertility process] could take years. You don't just go to a fertility specialist and get pregnant."

This statement paralyzed me with fear.

"Mom, maybe it's not God's plan for me to be a mother."

She replied by asking me, "Do you think it's God's plan to let drug addicts get pregnant? Do you think God is orchestrating all of this?"

I am not sure if those were rhetorical questions or just her sharing her frustration for me.

It took every courageous bone in my body to make an appointment at the fertility clinic. I knew many people wondered why I didn't go sooner. I look back and ask myself the same question. To be honest, I was scared of the results, scared they would tell me I could never have children.

Interestingly enough, I hadn't felt any fear when I prepared to learn my genetic test results for the BRCA1 gene mutation. I believe fear grows from knowing too much. As children, we are fearless. We jump off the bed and don't worry about getting hurt. As adolescents, we play sports competitively without being afraid of losing. As teenagers, we take the first sip of beer and never worry about the consequences. But fear grows with every failure and every consequence. I became afraid I would never be able to have the picture-perfect family I had always dreamed of having.

Looking back, it's ironic I was more afraid of not having children than I was of getting cancer. But I saw my mother survive this ill-fated disease, so I supposed I would too (had I had the gene). I did not, however, have any prior experience with infertility. This was a whole new ballgame. But at the same time, I had hope. I expected to get some answers.

Bryan and I went to our first appointment with a fertility

specialist and completed all of the recommended testing. Once the testing was completed and our results were in, we met with the doctor.

I expected answers but instead was met with a series of questions.

"Did anyone in your family have a hard time getting pregnant?"

"Did your mom have a hard time getting pregnant?"

"Do you have sisters who were able to conceive easily?"

I looked at the doctor and said, "What does my family have to do with what you know about *me*?"

I suspected she knew something I didn't know. The doctor had all of my paperwork and results from multiple fertility tests in front of her, so why was she asking me these questions? *I'm the one wanting answers.*

Not *If*, but WHEN?
Bridget

After learning I was a BRCA1 gene mutation carrier, I began to navigate the muddy waters of what to do next. From the moment I heard the word "carrier," I knew I would have my breasts removed. The question was not if, but when? I was the first person in our family who had time, albeit not a lot of time, but some time to research medical surveillance and surgical options. My mother, of course, never had time to make a decision because she got the cancer diagnosis before she'd had a chance to undergo mastectomy surgery. That is what I needed to avoid.

So, my parents and I went on a quest to determine how my health should be managed. My research about BRCA carriers and options for surveillance was sparse, so we reached out to the "experts." We interviewed many local breast surgeons and oncologists; we simply needed guidance on a good starting point for the health management of a genetic carrier.

Much to our surprise, many of these "experts" either had no clue about how to manage a gene carrier or, sadly, didn't seem to care. One oncologist even called me cancerphobic.

Of course, I am cancerphobic, you nitwit! My chances of developing breast cancer at a young age are 80-90%. I'm staring down the barrel of a loaded gun, and I am trying to be proactive about my health. You should be applauding me for my proactive measures instead of insulting me!

Another "expert" we consulted was Dr. E who studied tumor biology, biochemistry, radiology, and pathology at renowned institutions. Dr. E was the partner of the oncologist who treated my mother and was widely known for his work in genetics, cancer prevention, and risk assessment, and was even recently nationally recognized for his great work in genetic cancer research. He came recommended, from those who knew him, as a kind and compassionate man. What a perfect physician for me/us to consult and right at our doorstep. We felt so fortunate!

I still cannot understand what transpired at the appointment. There we sat, my parents and I, in a small exam room. After Dr. E entered the room and we made our introductions, my mother gave him a brief history of the generations of early deaths from cancer in our family and informed him of her own breast cancer diagnosis at age 32. Most importantly, we told him that I had just been diagnosed with the BRCA1 mutation.

My mother then stated, "We are here today to discuss the option of prophylactic mastectomies for our daughter, Bridget."

Really, we were seeking support. Any kind of support.

Help us save my life!

I talked, my mother talked, my dad even asked questions, and Dr. E had very little to say. At one point in the appointment Dr. E excused himself and stated he would be back. He returned with a calculator and did a few "calculations."

He then turned to me. "It is not necessary for you to have preventative surgery. You have no greater statistical chance than the general population of getting breast cancer."

We sat in shock and disbelief at what he said.

Did you not hear us when we said I carry the BRCA1 gene mutation?

Another oddity from this man was that he tried to argue my mother's genetic status, stating to her, "You, yourself, may not even be a BRCA1 mutation carrier."

We, again, stared at him in disbelief. Three out of the four children in my family tested positive for the BRCA gene mutation. Where is he suggesting it came from? It couldn't have been my father's side. There isn't a trace of breast cancer on his side of the family.

We wanted this renowned physician to confirm that prophylactic surgery was an option for me. That I *needed* this life-saving measure. What *was* Dr. E saying to me? Would he want to bury a daughter? A sister? A wife?

I can only speculate why Dr. E told me I was not at risk and that surgery at such a young age was unnecessary. I speculate he thought the risk of being socially unacceptable and emotionally damaged from having my breasts removed outweighed the risk of breast cancer. I speculate that, due to Dr. E's culture, which didn't hold women in very high regard, he thought I would be worthless as a female without natural breasts. Perhaps he viewed us as pathetic and desperate, I don't know. We left his office that day and vowed never to see Dr. E again. We knew he was wrong in the medical advice he gave us.

At first, we were discouraged by our visit with Dr. E, and for a short period of time, I felt lost. I wondered if any doctor would support my desire to be proactive. Would I have to relinquish my efforts to avoid cancer and just eventually succumb to it? Que Sera Sera?

Determined and resolute, I refused to be a ticking time bomb. I needed to find someone to help me save my life. Well, save me from a cancer diagnosis, at the very least.

At last, my mother found a local breast surgeon—Dr. J, the person we had been looking for. Dr. J is a beautiful Asian American woman, gentle and soft-spoken. She completely understands the seriousness of being a BRCA1 gene mutation carrier. At our first meeting she insisted on scheduling prophylactic mastectomies as soon as possible.

To my surprise, I suddenly felt hesitant.

Was I *really* ready for that?

I hadn't yet completely resigned myself to surgery. Even if I was going to, should I do it so soon, at the mere age of 21? I was single and getting ready to begin nursing school. Should I wait until after I got married and had children? But that could be in ten years; I could have already been a cancer victim by then.

Dr. J sensed my hesitation and suggested some ways we could keep a close eye on my breasts rather than rushing into surgery. Every six months I would have a mammogram and then six months later have a breast MRI. So, that is where we started.

I looked like such an anomaly walking into the breast center for my first mammogram. The questions. The stares. One woman with a short gray bob haircut and a periwinkle cardigan sat near me in the uncomfortable chairs. I guessed her to be in her 60s. I stared at the tacky floral painting on the waiting room wall opposite us. She kept sneaking looks at me out of the corner of her eye.

I know she wanted to ask, "What are you doing here?"

I wanted to whisper back, "Saving my life."

But we stayed silent.

I flipped through an old People Magazine, trying not to think about my breast being squished between two large plastic plates. Then they called my name, "Bridget Winn." The nurse took me to the changing area and asked me flat out, "What is your indication for this imaging?"

"I'm BRCA positive."

She nodded and jotted it down. I slipped on my soft pink gown and followed her into the mammogram room. Thankfully they didn't squeeze my 20-something, semi-small breasts too hard. I left that day feeling proud of myself for taking my first preventative steps against becoming a breast cancer victim.

Opening a worm of cans
Maureen

Maureen,
I am so sorry you have my cancer gene, but I am not sorry that I gave birth to you. Certainly, if we got to choose our problems in life, we would not choose each other's. We cannot choose what is dealt to us, but we can choose HOW we deal with what is dealt to us. Really, what options do we have? Life is very fragile and as you get older you will learn this all too well. My motto is work hard, play hard, and enjoy the good times to the fullest because you never know when you will get shit on, like we were on Friday. Knowledge is power. I love you.
MOM

Shortly after receiving my genetic test results on the previous Friday, I received this email from my mom. It was short, sweet, and to the point, just like her.

Although she has never been an overly affectionate mother, my mom has never ceased to show me her unconditional support, sometimes in subtle ways, like leaving my favorite cookies on the kitchen counter for me when I came home from college. It took me many years to understand that sometimes the smallest acts of thoughtfulness mean the most.

She showed her love in other ways, of course. Like by agreeing to run with me in the Chicago marathon of October 2008 when I convinced her it was a good idea for us to do one together. Honestly, I think she just wanted to be there to see me suffer through it, which is what happened. I can still see her literally running circles around me as I inched down the course—just so she could say she ran circles around me. But it is because of her that I have finished three marathons. It is also because of her that I will be a successful working mother. Because of her I will see it through when my marriage gets tough. It is because of my mother I make the cutest birthday cakes for my children, and it is because of her that I am creative enough to do so. It is because of my mother that I was born into this world and it is because of her research about our family's breast cancer history

45

and courage to speak up that I am able to live to pass these *wonderful* genes on to my children. Most women fear turning into their mothers. To me, it is the greatest achievement.

Part of becoming my mom meant marrying my dad. Not really. That would be weird. Our family is strange but not that kind of strange. I married someone very, very much like my father.

Somehow, I was fortunate enough to marry Josh, the tall, dark, handsome love of my life. We could not be more different. He is day, I am night. He is an early riser, and I am a night owl. He is a fiscally responsible banker; I am a creative and spontaneous marketer. He is an extremely realistic introvert, and I am a slightly paranoid extrovert. But over the last ten years, we have balanced each other out. We have started to rub off on each other, which means I occasionally get him out of his comfort zone, and he has taught me the joy of being boring.

Josh loves me—even at my ultimate worst—and that is something I can't even say about myself. He has taught me the meaning of unconditional love. I feel very fortunate to have married Josh. Unfortunately, for Josh, he chose to marry me. He makes it look easy although I will be the first to tell you, it's not. I often find myself thinking, *Sweet, sweet Josh.*

The hardest part about marriage is when I turn into a deranged monster over an insignificant detail in life, realize it is insignificant after yelling about it, and then switch back to loving wife within moments because I still want to make our dinner reservations without sounding bipolar.

For example, "I swear to God, if you put my dry-cleaning clothes in the laundry one more time! No, it is *not* fine. I am never talking to you again!" *Oh crap, we have dinner reservations in 20 minutes, which means we have to leave now...* "Are you ready, honey? We need to go. You look great in that suit, by the way!"

You should see the look on poor Josh's face. Fortunately, Josh is a quick learner. More likely than not, now he is more likely to say, "Okay, Maureen, let's go," rather than "What the F...?" *Sweet, sweet Josh.*

Another difficult thing about marriage is joining a new family, especially when the family is very different from your own. Josh's family is much more... mild... than mine. My family curses and talks about inappropriate things at dinner like hysterectomies and circumcisions. In my ten years of knowing Josh's family, I have never heard such topics discussed at their family functions. And, honestly, it's better that way. Josh came into our family and has not complained once. *Sweet, sweet Josh.*

I knew the future with Josh did not include real breasts, but I assumed it did guarantee babies. For many years I naively told myself that the BRCA1 gene mutation only lived in my breasts. What I had to accept was the gene actually lived in my DNA. It wasn't just my breasts that had to fight this battle. My ovaries—my baby makers—were in the fight as well.

I've been going to the doctor on a (semi) regular basis since my mother first told me to go at age 18.

When I was 22, I inquired about having a yearly CA-125 lab test drawn. CA-125 stands for Cancer Antigen 125. A CA-125 test detects a protein in the blood that may be produced in ovarian cancer. Developed in 1981, the CA-125 test is the most recommended screening tool for ovarian cancer. However, it is known for not being reliable because high levels may also be associated with conditions other than cancer, like a simple common cold, for example. Despite this, the test is still the most widely used biomarker for ovarian cancer.

The doctor with whom I'd requested the CA-125 responded in obvious disagreement with this surveillance measure.

"I wouldn't recommend the test; you are just opening up a can of worms."

I wanted to tell the doctor, "I am sure as shit glad my mother opened up a can of worms years ago, otherwise I would probably be seeing an oncologist right now to find out the current chemo recommendations instead of seeing you for the current preventative recommendations."

Instead, I called Bridget in a flutter and cried, "He told me

I'm opening up a *worm of cans*!!" She attempted to comfort me, but I can still hear her laughing on the other end of the phone.

I am blessed that every month, my period faithfully came three days early, usually in the morning, so I was always prepared. I never had any "women issues"—with my periods, my ovaries, nothing. Until, of course, the day I did.

For over a week, I had cramps bilaterally (you know you have the BRCA mutation when "bilateral" is a common term in your vocabulary), although worse on one side than the other. The dull and achy pain hurt into my hip and groin. The fact that pain was in my hip seemed odd to me, so I made an appointment with my primary care doctor.

Dr. W was a nice man and, after chatting for a few minutes, he assured me this was muscular. I told him my concern about the pain being caused by an ovarian cyst (or worse) and he said he was confident it was not. He hugged me (to me, a sign of him comforting a crazy patient) and left. I wasn't crazy, but I was anxious, and the appointment did not help ease my mind.

I couldn't stop thinking about the pain, so I took it upon myself to Google ovarian tumors. I knew self-diagnosing via the internet was a bad idea, but I was looking for relief. I found the opposite. Not only were my symptoms spot-on with an ovarian mass, I also found out I was dying. Did WebMD tell me that? No. Did I tell myself that? Yes.

Because I did not know the difference between ovarian cyst and ovarian cancer, I simply assumed the worst. I began to cry on my way home from work. I cried and I cried and I cried. I got home from work and I cried. Sweet, sweet Josh hugged me, and I cried even more. For the first time, I was scared.

And I was mad. For the first time, the reality of having the BRCA1 gene mutation smacked me hard.

Science, Little Swimmers, and Second Chances
Kathryn

The truth was, the infertility doctor did not have any answers for me or Bryan, who sat quietly beside me. I think she was hoping my family history would give her some insight into why we weren't able to get pregnant, but I didn't know anything about my family's history with fertility.

I told her about our family history with cancer, but she didn't think that had anything to do with why I wasn't getting pregnant. Plus, since I didn't have the BRCA gene mutation, it didn't play a role in this mystery either. The doctor briefly commented she was happy I understood the importance of genetic testing and how impactful it could be. In the back of my head, I questioned what this had to do with me not getting pregnant or why that even mattered in the conversation.

"Just please give me the results of my tests," I begged.

The doctor eventually began to explain. She did not tell us I was unable to have children or that I was infertile. What the doctor said was worse: I had "unexplained infertility." She continued on with her explanation without blinking an eye, as if this were completely normal. I doubt this doctor realized I was still stuck on the word "unexplained."

How could something be unexplained?
What happened to modern medicine?
I thought today's medicine could solve all problems!

As the doctor continued, she noted this was the worst kind of infertility *(no kidding)* because they could not find something to repair.

At that point, the recommendations from the doctor started coming fast and furious. I was overwhelmed. And if *I* was overwhelmed, I couldn't imagine what was going through Bryan's head.

I was afraid to look over at him as we sat at the little round table in the consultation room. Unfortunately, we would see that table—a little round table with a pen holder filled with nice silver and black pens labeled "Reproductive Resource Center"—at the fertility clinic for four more years. I always wondered who the heck would take one of those pens? It would be like advertising to the world you couldn't get pregnant. Every time we sat in that consultation room with its distinct latex smell, I stared at the detailed 3D diagram of a woman's uterus and reproductive organs and tried to imagine why my own parts didn't work.

Upon leaving this awful appointment, I immediately called my mom.

"Did you get pregnant easily? Do you know anyone in our family who struggled to conceive? Is there something you're not telling me?!"

"Slow down. Yes, your dad looked at me and I got pregnant. And, yes, actually, I have an aunt who never had children. Now that I say that, it seemed very strange, as we were from a large Catholic family. I am guessing she had fertility issues as well."

"Is this all you can tell me?"

"Yes, I'm sorry. This is all I know."

Just like the doctor, I, too, had wished I could find some answers in my family history. But there were none to be found. My mom claims everything is genetic, and I believe she's right. Unfortunately, true infertility testing and treatments didn't come about until after the death of my great-aunt who couldn't conceive. The first IVF baby (test tube baby[xii]) was actually born just prior to me being born. So, even if a genetic link existed between my mom's aunt and me that affected our inability to conceive, we had no way to determine it.

After reviewing the doctor's recommendations, Bryan and I decided to begin with artificial inseminations. Artificial insemination is a simple procedure. On the appropriate date of a woman's cycle, the doctor inserts sperm from the man into the woman's uterus and then we all hope those little swimmers find their way to the egg.

Bryan only had one job with artificial insemination. He

had to provide the sperm. He would wake up, "retrieve" his sample (I'll spare you the details), hand the plastic jar with the sample to me, which I held next to my body to keep at body temperature, and then he showered quickly. Bryan then put the sample in between his waist and pants while he drove the sample over to the clinic. The sample had to be kept at body temperature and had to arrive at the clinic one hour earlier than I did. So Bryan would leave his sample at the clinic, where they stored it in a warmer, come home, and pick me up. I secretly laugh inside at how importantly he took his one, teeny, weeny job.

Sadly, three artificial inseminations did not work. After much debate, many long conversations, and quite a few tears we decided to move on to in-vitro fertilization (IVF). Bryan and I learned the chances of getting pregnant with IVF are about 50%.[xiii] I was convinced IVF would work and that our time was *finally* here.

It took a lot to convince Bryan to try IVF. Not only was it extremely expensive and time consuming, but also Bryan wondered why we would "force" ourselves to get pregnant. His theory was *If it was supposed to happen, it would happen.* Que Sera Sera, I guess. His point was valid, but I had a hard time accepting it.

And, so we began our first round of IVF with a series of doctor appointments, drugs, blood tests, more appointments, and finally the egg retrieval. We had 12 eggs removed and fertilized with Bryan's sperm. We were over the moon excited!

Bryan brought me home from the egg retrieval and the doctor's orders were to take the pain medication and go to bed. The discharge instructions clearly stated that someone must stay with me for the rest of the day. However, I felt fine, probably due to the pain medication, so I sent Bryan back to work. I woke up a few hours later with excruciating pain in my abdomen and horrendous nausea.

I called Bryan to come home. The pain worsened, so bad that when I took a deep breath sharp pain spread all over my body. Bryan called the doctor's office to see if this was normal. They said it was and prescribed me some more nausea medication.

This was normal? I knew it was *not* normal, but I tried to ignore it and went to bed.

As Bryan and I lay in bed, the pain continued to get worse.

"The pain feels worse when I lay down. It feels like a ton of bricks are sitting on my chest."

"Maybe you should try sleeping sitting up?"

In tears, I tried to comply.

Finally, at 11:00 p.m. I couldn't bear a single second more of the pain, so I begged Bryan to drive me to the emergency room. After we checked in, Bryan sat in the waiting room nonchalantly reading the newspaper, a look of pure boredom blended with a hint of annoyance on his face. I waited in the cold hospital room wearing only a gown when a nurse came by to apologize about the wait.

"The doctors must visit the more urgent cases first."

I wasn't sure if it was the pain, my irritated husband, or my lack of clothing that finally put me over the edge. Tears rolled from my eyes as I clutched my abdomen, when the ER doctor finally came in.

I quickly explained. "We are in the process of doing IVF and I had an egg retrieval earlier today. I am concerned something has gone wrong."

"I've seen women in here the day of an egg retrieval before and typically they just have anxiety over if it will work or not. How are you feeling about IVF? Do you think you are just having some anxiety?" he uttered carelessly.

"How am I feeling?!?!?! Currently, my pain is an 85 on a scale of 1-10. I feel *fine* with the IVF process. This is something else!" I cried.

The doctor begrudgingly agreed to do an x-ray of my abdomen.

The x-ray tech gasped at what he saw, calling for a doctor immediately. The first available ER doc rushed in. As he glanced at my x-ray, he exclaimed in a hurried voice, "We've got a problem. Blood is filling up your abdomen and pushing on your lungs. We need to get you into surgery immediately."

Now I had anxiety.

It was so serious they took me by ambulance to another hospital for emergency surgery. As I was wheeled to the ambulance, I had a significant amount of pain medication on board and was feeling fantastic about life. We passed the doctor who had accused me of anxiety, and I waved. What I really wanted to do was yell out, "Who the hell put MD behind your name?!" I also wanted to say something of equal meanness to my husband who told me to just sleep sitting up. But the sedation settled in and I eventually passed out.

As I went into surgery my husband waited, this time less annoyed. My poor husband had to follow the ambulance, call our families, and ended up not sleeping for almost 48 hours. When I came out of surgery, he apologized for not taking my pain more seriously.

As I recovered in the hospital, my reproductive endocrinologist stopped by.

"It appears your ovary was punctured while the eggs were being taken out," she explained with absolutely no ownership whatsoever.

"My ovary was punctured by *you*, as *you* were removing the eggs," I stated, making it clear who was to blame. *As if I didn't have enough fertility problems, the doctor stabbed one of my ovaries!*

"This is very rare and should not affect your fertility moving forward."

The hell it's not. My husband wasn't exactly elated about doing IVF from the get-go.

Dread and great sadness consumed me. I feared we would not be able to move forward with the transfer. Infertility treatments, much like our procreation vacation, were getting off to a rough start.

Luckily, the fertility specialist agreed to transfer two of

our 12 frozen embryos when I was healed. She gave us more to consider when she said, "Your embryos look great. We will transfer two of the best-looking ones. But, if you really want to be sure we get the best chance of success, you can do genetic testing, also known as Preimplantation Genetic Diagnosis (PGD), on those embryos."

"What does that mean exactly?"

"We remove a few cells from each of the frozen embryos and send them out to a lab that will test the chromosomes for abnormalities. If any of the embryos come back abnormal, we will not use them. We will only transfer the embryos that have normal chromosomal data."

I had heard about PGD before, but not in terms of increasing our chances of a successful pregnancy. PGD testing was being used to identify and prevent passing along certain defects in embryos. More than 100 genes can be identified in PGD testing and one of those genes is BRCA.[xiv] If I'd had the BRCA gene mutation and did not want to pass it on to a future child, I had the option to eliminate this embryo. Science is fascinating.

Although, destroying embryos that carry the BRCA mutation walks a fine ethical line, in my humble opinion. Regrettably, BRCA is a part of our family. At the same time, I don't regret how our BRCA journey has shaped who we are and how we live our lives. The chance to remove this for future children was something I couldn't quite wrap my mind around. However, if we could use PGD testing to determine why we were not getting pregnant or to increase our chances, then I was up for it.

Unfortunately, PGD testing would also extend the process by a few months and a few thousand dollars. The conversation with Bryan about PDG testing was short.

"No."

He went on. "There is no reason to believe this transfer is not going to work. Let's just stay the course."

The good news is I survived the punctured ovary. The bad news is IVF did not work. Convincing Bryan to do IVF a second time would not be easy.

Not Mine to Keep
Bridget

A few days after my first mammogram, the results displayed suspicious spots on my right breast. Immediately, Dr. J ordered a breast MRI. Within a day of the results of my mammogram, I was strapped face down on a board and rolled into an MRI tube. I never considered myself a claustrophobic until then (and one time later in life when I hid in a trunk while playing hide-and-go-seek with my children). Fighting back nausea, claustrophobia, and now panic of feeling trapped in a tube of death, I was terrified of what the results might show.

Holding the remote with the panic button tightly in my right hand, I told myself, "Go to your happy place, Bridget."

Then it became an internal battle. *Where is my happy place?! I don't have one!*

Somehow, I made it through without hitting the panic button, but the panic didn't completely go away as we waited for the MRI results.

The MRI revealed that not only were the suspicious spots still there, they were even more alarming on the MRI imaging. Dr. J called and stated she was very concerned about the spots. Promptly, Dr. J ordered an ultrasound-guided punch biopsy. A punch biopsy was guided by an ultrasound to locate the exact area to biopsy. She made an appointment for me that very afternoon for the procedure.

My mom, Maureen, and Kathryn met me at the breast center. They sat and held my hand during the whole procedure. After the radiologist punched three holes in my right breast with what looked like a small hole puncher, she handed me a box of Kleenex and said, "I'm sorry," implying, "You have cancer."

Her sympathy came from what she had seen on the breast ultrasound while doing the ultrasound punch biopsies. What she saw mimicked that of a malignancy. At the same time, I also had enlarged lymph nodes in my right armpit. The radiologist explained we would have to wait for the official results of the biopsy, but this was likely a breast malignancy and it had already spread.

If it was going to happen to anyone, it was going to happen to me. I was only 22 years old, but a BRCA1 gene mutation carrier. I left the appointment in shock.

How has this already happened?

When we arrived at home, I walked into my parents' house and saw my dad standing in our kitchen. I stumbled into his arms and cried. He cried, too. I can only imagine his thoughts. He watched his wife go through the trauma of breast cancer many years ago. Did he have to watch his daughter endure it, too?

After several terrifying days, the results of my punch biopsy pathology came back. Miraculously, the pathology came back clean! Dr. J could hardly believe it herself, so she immediately ordered another breast MRI. This time though, she wanted an MRI-guided biopsy. Her thought was that maybe the ultrasound-guided biopsy didn't actually biopsy the right spots.

So back into the MRI tube I went. I was face down in the tube again, this time fighting back panic *and* fearing the pain of the MRI needle-guided biopsy. During this procedure, they would place a needle directly in the suspicious area and take a sample of the tissue. I was under no anesthesia. My teeth were clenched the whole time and I grasped the plastic panic button so tight I had to peel my fingers off of it when the MRI was finished. After several tense moments in the MRI, I felt the table slide back out of the tube. But there had been no needle biopsy.

The MRI tech came into the room and said they couldn't find anything to biopsy. There was nothing there! The suspicious spots that had caused my life to flash before my eyes were suddenly gone. Another tech then took me immediately into an ultrasound room to look for the spots on my breast. Again, nothing there. Everyone was shocked. The spots that showed up on a mammogram, MRI, and ultrasound had completely disappeared.

My mom proclaimed that it was divine intervention. I didn't care what it was; all I knew was that I wanted my breasts off and I wanted them off as soon as possible. I was not going to put myself or my family through that again.

I visited with Dr. J again shortly after the "scare." I was becoming a regular in her office. The staff knew me by my first name when I walked in. This shouldn't have been a surprise to me. I imagine I was the only 22-year-old patient they had.

I didn't need to explain to Dr. J why screening wasn't working out for me. As fun as it was to have a mammogram, two MRIs, three punch biopsies and my life flash before my eyes, it wasn't something I was going to endure annually until I had the inevitable surgery. I was ready to have my breasts removed.

I had no doubt in my mind it was time. We scheduled my mastectomy just a short time later in December of 2005.

Prior to my mastectomy, I can't remember any anxiety over what my body was going to look like after the surgery. Although, I do remember looking at mastectomy pictures on the internet in efforts to prepare myself. Considering everything that had happened the year prior with the cancer scare, I wasn't really concerned about the outcome of my body. I was also not attached to my breasts like some women are. I knew deep down that they were never mine to keep. More importantly, they had the ability to threaten my life. They were goners and I was ready.

I felt in good spirits the morning of the surgery. I even took pictures of the "originals" as my mom encouraged me to do so. I asked Maureen to take the pictures, but she declined in near disgust. I was forced to take a boob selfie (you know, before it was a thing.)

I didn't feel any sadness the day of the double mastectomy; I did, however, shed several tears when my dad started to cry before I went into surgery. I understood why he was so emotional, but to me it was somewhat of a victory. I was there by choice, and not because I was being forced to have my breasts removed from a cancer ridden body.

In all honesty, I was mostly concerned about the giant zit that had erupted on my forehead the day prior. All I could think was *I am about to go into surgery with a super cute plastic surgeon and I have an enormous pimple on my face.* This pimple was not a threat to my health going into surgery; it was a threat to my self-image. I was still a 22-year-old girl concerned with my looks. I am certain the doctor didn't care about the way I looked. He was, after all, about to remove my breasts.

As I was prepped in the preoperative area, a minister from my parents' church said a prayer with my family. I hugged my parents and whispered to my mom that if anything unexpected happened during surgery and I was left a vegetable, to pull the plug. She thanked me for making my wishes clear (seriously). I was then wheeled into the operating room.

Still then, I felt no sense of nervousness or sadness. I was just numb... only because they keep those operating rooms so cold. The cold made my nipples stand straight up for the last time. I think they were giving me one final salute. *So long, old friends.*

After getting a couple of warm blankets from the nurse and some good drugs, I was ready. Things got hazy and before I completely went to sleep, I wondered if any of the staff found me or my situation peculiar. It really didn't matter. Then things got a little hazier and I told my plastic surgeon how handsome he was. Then I was out. And they were gone.

Scared but Never Alone
Maureen

I could handle a mastectomy, I could handle never breast-feeding, I could handle the risk that I could still develop breast cancer, but I could *not* handle ovarian cancer. And after my research online, I was convinced that's exactly what I had. I was dying, I was sure of it.

Ovarian cancer would destroy my hope for children. Like Kathryn, I wanted babies! Lots of babies! The thought of a gene mutation affecting my ovaries was new and terrifying. I was mad I had this stupid, stupid gene.

Why? Why do I have it!? This is too fucking hard. I should have been more proactive. I should have done more, I scolded myself.

Josh sat with me while I inconsolably cried. He told me that we would get through this together... sweet, sweet Josh.

I couldn't stop thinking about ovarian cancer throughout the next workday. Finally, I told a coworker. Emily and I had been classmates at Creighton together and, upon graduation, accepted similar jobs at ConAgra Foods within the same division. We started on the same day and for five years we sat just two desks from each other. Over the years, Emily had become a good friend—as the Golden Girls would say, a pal and a confidante. I have found that work relationships are a unique type of relationship. I spent more time with my coworkers than my husband and inevitably ended up telling them more than my best friends. I believe this was due to close proximity.

With Emily it was also because we were more similar than different. We both graduated from Creighton in May 2009 (Emily a little smarter than me), we both were good Catholic girls (Emily a little more Catholic than me), we both married young and daydreamed about quitting our jobs to stay home with our three fictional children (due to unforeseen corporate bullshit, Emily before me), and we were both a little crazy (me a little more than Emily). Which is why she didn't even blink before responding, "Don't do anything! I will research this for you."

Incredibly intelligent and driven, Emily is great at talking people off the ledge. She knew that if I started Googling it again, I would certainly jump. She advocated for me when I couldn't do it myself. She sat at her computer and researched my symptoms. Then she started sending me messages to help calm my fears. She messaged me pieces of articles reassuring me these menstrual pains were normal. Almost all premenopausal women have them. The pain I had was exactly that. I would, indeed, live.

Within no time, a weight lifted off my shoulders. Emily was supporting me the way my sisters had so often done. Which is when I realized, *My sisters! My mom! Why had I not called them to tell them I was sure I had ovarian cancer?*

I knew why. It would have made my craziness real. I didn't want them to worry about something that did not yet exist. I never wanted to say to my mom, "I have ovarian cancer."

So I made an appointment with my gynecologist. Sweet, sweet Josh came with me and held my hand. After an ultrasound with my doctor telling the tech to "measure that, measure that, zoom in there, zoom in further, further" and me imagining them measuring the mass that was growing on my ovary, the doctor said, "Everything looks good, thanks."

What was the pain? Who knows. It may have been a tiny ovarian cyst. It could have been muscular, like Dr. W had suspected. What I did know is that I didn't want it to be something I could have prevented.

I was 22 and it was becoming clear to me that it was time for me to start taking some preventative steps to reduce my risk of cancer, just as Bridget had done when she was my age.

First, I will address my risk of breast cancer and then my ovaries, I told myself. Since breast cancer was more likely to develop at a younger age, I knew I should start there.

Like Bridget and my mom, I thought the world of Bridget's breast surgeon, Dr. J. Kind and patient, she always made me feel comfortable with the unknown future that lay ahead of me. I started seeing her annually after I found out I was positive, and I always felt slightly proud every time I walked into her office. Not because I thought I was better than the average 60-year-old woman who generally filled her waiting room —but because I knew if I wasn't there as a 20-something BRCA1 gene mutation carrier, I certainly wouldn't have the luxury of being there as a 60-year-old woman.

Most appointments in Dr. J's office took five to ten minutes tops. That is, if nothing was wrong.

One particular appointment took much longer. It was the appointment I never wanted to have. The one I always wanted to avoid. Dr. J felt something during my annual appointment. She was shocked I hadn't felt it, which instantly made me think it must be a huge lump, at least stage 4. *If my mom had stage 2 at 32, surely, I could have stage 4 at 22.* The look on Dr. J's face sent anxiety running through my body. She ordered an ultrasound to immediately follow my appointment. Terrified, I called my mother. As I waited for her to drive to meet me, I paced the halls of the doctor's office in a fog of worry. *This was it,* I told myself. *This is how it happens.*

Twenty minutes later, I lay in the cold ultrasound room holding my breath and my mother's hand. When I had pictured what my first ultrasound would be like, the gel would have been about 12 inches lower and they would have been looking for a baby, not a lump.

PART IV: ROCK BOTTOM'S BASEMENT

It's dark down here.

Harsh Reality
Kathryn

The fight began on our way to Houston to visit Bryan's family. I was ready to turn around and do IVF again the very next month. Bryan was not (shocker).

"I don't think we should do this again anytime soon. You need time to heal."

Thoughts raced through my head.

What? Does he know who he married?! I am a bulldog. I'm tough. I can handle this. I am getting older by the day, time is slipping through the cracks, we are never going to have a family.

I took a few deep breaths and calmly explained that I had healed just fine from the surgery. He told me that was not what he meant.

When we landed in Houston, I had puffy eyes and was not speaking to Bryan. My in-laws could see something was wrong, and after our brief explanation, they agreed with Bryan that I should let my emotions heal before attempting IVF again. For all of my adult life, I had made my own decisions. Now these people in my life were telling me what I should and should not feel and do. I was livid and sad at the same time.

Yes, I was hurting, disappointed that IVF did not work. I was also high on hormones that were being injected into my body. My way of dealing with tough things in life is to just keep moving forward. One inch, one foot, one hour at a time. For me, the pain was not so unbearable if I could keep moving forward. *Why couldn't anyone understand that?*

The somber truth is, they were right. I needed time to heal emotionally and come to terms with infertility. As my mom had said at the beginning, it was not going to be a quick fix.

Deep down, I felt heartbroken, out of place. No one understood, most importantly not even my own husband. Our friends who were already parents kept telling us to "just enjoy our time together." I will never utter those words to anyone. Every time someone said that to us, I wanted to punch the culprit in the throat. I began hating people. But it wasn't their fault. They didn't know the pain I was feeling. The hardest part was that this bulldog didn't have any control in the outcome of the infertility treatments.

On top of being heartbroken, my marriage began to crumble. Bryan and I had two different perspectives on our infertility. His perspective was Que Sera Sera, whatever will be will be. Mine was the exact opposite. I was ready to fight to the death, to do anything and everything it took to make this happen.

Many years later, while sitting in church with our two little children, we heard a message that said, "Work like it depends on you, pray like it depends on God." *Thanks, Big Man. Where was that message years ago?* It resonated with Bryan and he apologized for the pain he put me through. In the end, we were able to grow from the experience and we developed a stronger marriage.

Somehow, some way, I convinced Bryan to move forward. We eventually went on to do a second round of IVF, which failed. We then pushed on and endured a third round.

While going through the third round of IVF, loaded with hormone medications and shot up like a chicken being plumped up for sale, I saw a Facebook post from a friend entitled "harsh reality." Her harsh reality was the fact that her three-year-old was up until 3:00 a.m., her newborn woke at 4:00 a.m., and then her alarm clock rang at 5:00 a.m. for work. I wanted to respond to the post what my harsh reality was at that time. I would have defined it as five years of infertility, three failed attempts at artificial insemination and two failed IVF cycles. *Harsh Reality!* Thankfully I refrained from posting a comment I would later regret. Plus, it was not her fault that my harsh reality was different from hers. What people do not realize is that infertility not only affects you but those around you. Going through this grief affected my relationships with others and my marriage.

I did have a few people in my life who completely understood my anguish; they too have unfortunately been in the same situation. A good friend struggled with infertility as well. After five years, three IVF treatments and two fertility clinics, they finally had two beautiful, healthy baby girls. When one of our rounds of IVF failed, she wrote me a long note with details about times she struggled and even included a prayer she wrote the baby she desperately wanted to conceive. Her note touched my life in ways that many people could not have done.

Hi Kathryn,

My heart aches for you right now. I have been in your shoes. Many nights I would cry myself to sleep, begging God to help us get pregnant. It felt nearly impossible. My body ached in pain from all of the shots, my heart broke into pieces every time a friend would announce their pregnancy. I've been right where you are, and I am telling you this because I want you to know you are not alone. I am not sure if this will help you or not, but I've included the prayer I prayed every night until the day our daughter was born. It helped give me hope.

"Dear Jesus, help me find peace in my struggle. Help me understand that your plan is far greater than my plan. I pray that you bless me with a life that is far more important than my own. I will treasure the life you give to me with all my heart. Whatever your will is, Jesus, please show that to me so that I may have peace in this process.

Love, S.

At times, the pain I felt from not being able to bring a life into this world made it difficult for me to breathe. It robbed me of simple joys like celebrating when my friends had babies and enjoying the sweet sound of a cooing baby. Even holding a baby in my arms was a painful reminder that I couldn't conceive.

But above it all, I had my life to live. My mom survived cancer, and my siblings were in the midst of dealing with being BRCA carriers. Even though I couldn't bring a life into this world, at least I wasn't suffering from the fear of losing my own. Struggling with infertility isn't life threatening. You could argue that there are far worse things to deal with, like cancer, something that could take your life.

Trying to get pregnant was not going to take away my life but it certainly took the life out of me. The doctor's appointments, shots, medications, mood swings, arguing about what our next steps should be, playing havoc with my career—it was all extremely draining.

I was a living Jekyll and Hyde. Because of the medications, my hormones fluctuated all over the place. To make matters worse, to get the best results with IVF I needed to avoid alcohol. Alcohol was the one thing that helped me relax. Not the healthiest of habits, I know, but a glass or two of my favorite Cabernet allowed me to shut off my brain and emotions for a much-needed break.

The holidays made avoiding alcohol at Christmas parties damn near impossible. Lots of parties. Lots of drinking. Lots of fun. None of which was I up for.

"Hey Kathryn, you are not a very fun person, are you?" said a new (and very drunk) neighbor at a particularly wild Christmas party. "Why don't you loosen up and have a drink?"

"You're an asshole."

I announced it matter-of-factly over the loud music and intoxicated partygoers. He looked at me, perplexed. But he was drunk and stupid, and I'm not even sure he heard me. At that moment, I knew I needed to leave before I unleashed my anger at other people. And the reality was, I *wasn't* fun. He was right.

Then, just when you think you've hit rock bottom, life takes one more swing at you.

Flat and Gone
Bridget

My breasts were gone. The day after my prophylactic double mastectomy, my mother helped me gather my IV and tubes as I shuffled gingerly to the bathroom in my hospital room. I stood in front of the mirror staring at myself for a few minutes. My disheveled hair, my pale skin, my squinty and slanted eyes—all displayed my exhaustion from the events of the day before.

Ugh, look at me, I thought to myself.

Give yourself a break, Bridget, my mind whispered. *You just had major surgery.*

Holding my breath, I gently pulled open the top of my hospital gown and peeked down at my chest where my perfect 22-year-old breasts used to be. For some reason, I was not surprised by the way my chest looked after having my breasts removed. My chest looked just what I had expected it to look like—flat and gone. Two horizontal, bright red incisions held together by black sutures and covered by steri-strips spread across my chest. (Truth be told, I was more horrified years later by the way my obliterated vagina looked after my babies were born. Talk about shock. Even the OB told me not to look. I should have listened to her.)

Under my skin, where my breasts used to be, lay small, hard breast expanders that would eventually be injected with saline to gradually stretch the skin. A pain pump coiled for pain control burrowed under my skin. JP tubes for drainage extended from either side of my missing breasts to drain extra fluid. The drain tubes were the biggest nuisance, but the pain pump was fabulous. However, narcotics slow down the gut and antibiotics breed vaginal yeast. I wish there had been a pump to ease constipation agony and the yeast infection from hell.

A few years later, I found a picture taken about two weeks after my mastectomy. My succession of thoughts was as follows:

1) Look at the size of my eyebrows!
2) Dang, I was skinny!
And...
3) I look happy.

As my mom, sisters, and I looked at the photo together, I commented on my caterpillar eyebrows. My mom was flabbergasted that, of all things, my first comment about the photo of that life-altering day was the thickness of my eyebrows. (In my defense, I do have super thick eyebrows that actually connect hairline to hairline. I inherited this trait from my father. Thanks, Dad.)

The mastectomy wasn't the horrifying experience that many people may assume it is. I experienced minimal pain or discomfort, and I was lucky to not have any complications. Most of my discomfort came from the inability to sleep on my stomach. My pain pump and JP tubes were removed about one week after surgery. I was out and about quickly after that.

My parents strongly encouraged me to try to be normal.

"Go out, have fun!"

I took their advice, too literally I'm afraid, and went out with my friends on New Year's Eve, a mere two weeks after my major surgery. A young girl, hopped up on pain meds, should not be consuming alcohol. The night was hazy (to say the least). I called my sister Kathryn around 10:00pm, speaking gibberish, and by 10:30, my dad was pulling me out of a downtown bar. I did my best to erase the memory forever, until my sisters mentioned "The New Year's Eve on painkillers" in their wedding toast to me a few years later. I avoided eye contact with my mother-in-law for quite some time after that. Thanks, sisters.

A perk to being a 22-year-old, healthy, cancer-free, mastectomy patient is that I was back on my feet in no time and ready to begin a rigorous nursing program. I started nursing school one month after my surgery.

I made many new friends in my program and slowly shared details with them about my surgery. I had no choice but to share my story with at least one of the girls because she was my assessment partner. During our first semester in the program we had to perform head-to-toe assessments on one another and while breast exams were not part of this, I felt it necessary she know why my body looked a little funny in a gown. She was perfectly wonderful and accepting about the situation, which was very comforting.

During my time at nursing school, I was having my expanders slowly injected with saline until they were the size of my choice. My plastic surgeon insisted I go larger than I was before. He was used to dealing with women who wanted larger breasts. That is, after all, why most young women have plastic surgery. All I wanted to be was as close as possible to the originals. A perfect B. Standing 5' 3" tall, (fine... 5' 2"), and 116 pounds, I knew I wasn't going to carry a double D well. That petite B cup suited me just fine.

I had to keep the hard expanders in until the summertime while I was on break from nursing school. Once the expanders stretched my skin sufficiently enough, I would have exchange surgery. Soft, more natural-looking silicone implants would replace the firm expanders.

As the semester ended and I neared replacement surgery, the expanders were quite rigid, looking very full. At the time, I was newly dating a guy, and we were out with his friends one night. I had just returned from the bathroom when I overheard them talking about me.

"No way, man!" said my date.

"Dude, I've seen fake ones before, and they are totally fake," his friend replied.

At that moment, they both turned and looked up to see me standing there. I simply smiled and sat down.

This wasn't just a boob job, silly boys.

However, I had no good reason to divulge my secrets. As far as my date goes, he never made it far enough to find out the truth.

Saying Ta-ta to my TaTas
Maureen

I lay on the ultrasound table, terrified, squeezing my mom's hand. I was too terrified to feel relief when the ultrasound tech said the lump in my breast that Dr. J detected was just a fatty nodule—in other words, nothing.

What? Fat? Fat is what scared the life out of me?

Oh, hell no! Those babies, my breasts, had to go, pronto.

When I had finally chosen to learn my genetic results, I was 21 and focused on starting a career and getting married. My mother had always said it was best to have a mastectomy before I had kids, which I planned to still be many, many years off. On the other hand, now two years later at age 23, I didn't have a reason to wait any longer for surgery. I was ready to start my adult life, and this was a big part of it. My lump scare sealed the deal. I refused to be a sitting duck, waiting for a cancer diagnosis.

It was time for my prophylactic double mastectomy.

I had always planned to have my breasts removed. However, prior to the fatty nodule, I hadn't been in a rush. I had told my friends in high school about my plans to have a mastectomy if I was BRCA1 positive, but "it would be great because it was like a free boob job." Silly, silly Maureen. While there are perks of a mastectomy, I would certainly never compare it to a "boob job."

There are visible similarities between a mastectomy and subsequent breast reconstruction to a "boob job," or more appropriately, breast augmentation surgery. While the final outcome may look the same to the unknowing eye, the surgeries are very, very different. Breast augmentation is cosmetic, primarily for the purpose of making a woman's breasts fuller or sometimes smaller. The surgery can be outpatient and the recovery time is usually a few short weeks. Also, the scars are undetectable. Typically, the scar can be found under the breast, with an implant being inserted above the breast tissue.

Breast reconstruction, on the other hand, varies greatly from cosmetic breast augmentation. Typically, breast reconstruction is the result of a mastectomy due to cancer, or the threat of it. When a woman undergoes a mastectomy and breast reconstruction, all the breast tissue is removed from her breast. Removing the nipple is optional. This procedure, called nipple-sparing mastectomy, leaves the nipple and areola intact, along with the breast skin, while all of the breast tissue underneath is removed.[xv] However, since the nipple contains vulnerable breast tissue, most women and their doctors choose to have the nipples removed as well. *Why take the risk?*

In breast reconstruction, the implants are inserted and placed on the chest wall, underneath the pectoral muscle. This may result in a loss of range of motion and strength. The recovery process can be very long, sometimes several months to a year, depending on the type of reconstruction. Also, because the tissue within the breast is removed, breastfeeding is not possible and most of the feeling to the area is lost.

Learning the ins and outs, literally, of breast reconstruction can be overwhelming—especially in your early 20s. I gathered all the confidence I could muster and decided to start meeting with doctors.

Although choosing to have a prophylactic mastectomy is a big decision, thankfully Bridget had already made many of the crucial decisions for me. She picked out wonderful doctors who had made her recovery process seamless. I also decided to use Dr. J as my breast surgeon. She was arguably the best breast surgeon and has, sadly for other women currently needing mastectomies, since retired.

I did, however, choose to find a different plastic surgeon, no matter how handsome Bridget thought hers was. At the time, Bridget was having rippling around her breast implants. I joined her at a post-op appointment and when she expressed her rippling concern to the plastic surgeon, he said it was a side effect of implants because she was so thin.

Well, shit, I thought to myself. *We're the same size and that's not the look I'm going for.*

So I did some doctor hunting of my own.

Truthfully, I only met with one other plastic surgeon. Dr. R must have impressed me, because despite the implant leaking when he let me feel one, I chose him. He reassured me they won't leak once they are implanted, but I fear that may have foreshadowed my future. In general, silicone implants have a life of roughly 10-20 years.[xvi] Doctors typically caution patients that they will likely have reconstruction at some point in their lives. But one problem at a time, please.

There are several types of reconstruction to consider after a mastectomy and navigating the options can be overwhelming. Expander implants (like Bridget's surgery) and direct-to-implants (DTI) are two of the most common types of reconstruction.[xvii] A DTI breast reconstruction replaces the breast with an implant right away at the time of surgery.

Other types include Latissimus Dorsi flap, TRAM flap, DIEP flap, TUG flap, and GAP flap. The "flap" refers to a flap of skin and/or fat that is removed from one portion of your body (back, belly, buttocks, or other part of the body) to be used to create breast implants.[xviii] Sexy, right? TRAM flap surgery removes a portion of the abdomen to reconstruct breasts. This is the most common type of flap surgery because, as it turns out, our belly jiggle is a lot like our breast jiggle. (Side note: I'm not a doctor and cannot confirm that doctors technically refer to it as jiggle.)

For me, the reconstruction process was easy after a series of quick decisions. I was determined in my decision to have surgery and more focused on saving my life than how I looked.

Dr. R gave me the option to do an immediate reconstruction with implants, rather than the expanders that Bridget used. With immediate reconstruction, the plastic surgeon places the implants in during the initial surgery. This means one surgery, instead of the two or more you would have with delayed reconstruction. It also means a quicker recovery, again because there is only one surgery. This sounded like a good choice for me. I lived in Chicago at the time, although I was having my surgery in Kansas City where my family lived. I was able to stay in Kansas City for two weeks for my recovery, not enough time to fill my expanders if I chose delayed reconstruction. So I chose to do the immediate reconstruction with implants.

However, immediate reconstruction can be a difficult procedure because the skin must be stretched over the new implants. My doctor warned me he would try to do immediate reconstruction, but he couldn't guarantee it.

With the doctors and details in place, all I had to do was schedule the surgery. Friday, October 13, was the first available date. Friday the 13th. Sure, why the hell not?

Sweet, sweet Josh was there, holding my hand, as I lay in a hospital bed, prepped to have my breasts removed before we were even married. My family surrounded me, and I think someone had requested a priest be there, adding to an already morbid scene.

As they wheeled me off to surgery, a nurse said carelessly, "It is Friday the 13th. I hope you aren't superstitious."

I muttered, "I'm not superstitious but I am a little-stitious," channeling my inner Michael Scott, and then I blacked out.

I woke up from surgery as I was being wheeled into my recovery room. My parents and sisters were there by my side from that moment until I was wheeled out of the hospital.

Although heavily drugged, I clearly remember a nurse waking me up the night after surgery and saying, "Excuse me ma'am, what did you have surgery for?"

If you know me in the slightest, you know you don't wake me up, ever. I like my sleep. And I hate when it's interrupted. The death glare I shot the nurse was enough for her to answer the question herself.

"A mastectomy. Oh yeah, that's right," she said in a cherry voice as she went about her business.

I get it, it would be a little confusing to see a 23-year-old woman recovering from a mastectomy. But also, there is no need to make me feel more self-conscious about this decision than necessary.

Thankfully, I came out of surgery with my *foobs* (fake boobs) in place. Immediate reconstruction worked out well for me. However, prior to my surgery, Dr. R and I had talked about cup size. In all honesty, I wanted to have smaller breasts than my natural size. I am a petite person and always felt like my size C breasts were not proportional to my body. Unfortunately, when I woke up from surgery, my plastic surgeon informed me that I was still a C. Because my body was designed for a C, he claimed, that is what would look best post-surgery. *Sure, whatever.* I didn't get the petite ballerina-shaped body I desired, but I was okay with that. A female coworker once told me I will appreciate having curves when I am older. I'm still waiting.

Battered but Undaunted
Kathryn

Our doctor had recommended Preimplantation Genetic Diagnosis (PGD) during our first round of IVF. Possible candidates for genetic testing include: carriers of gene and chromosome disorders, women over the age of 35, women experiencing recurrent pregnancy loss, and women with more than one failed infertility treatment.

Although I qualified as a candidate, we still wrestled with medical, financial and even ethical concerns. Bryan felt skeptical, like we were "playing God." I was thankful for the astounding amount of information that could be gleaned from genetic testing—the knowledge our family had gained from genetic testing was literally saving the lives of my sisters and many other women around the world—even so, I never expected to be walking down the genetic testing road again. We'd paid so many expensive fees already and the path ahead wouldn't come cheap.

Also, too much information could have controversial impacts, such as the ability to pick the sex of the embryo or eliminate any sort of genetic defect. I didn't know how I felt about having the option to design our future family. Designer handbags and designer babies, along with hefty price tags, have become the future of the world.

I finally verbalized the question that tipped the scales in my favor: "If you knew there was a way to solve, fix, or even impact a potential problem, would you pursue it?"

Our hope, battered but undaunted, pushed us forward. After weeks of discussion, research, and meeting with a genetic counselor, Bryan and I decided to move forward with PGD testing.

As we headed into genetic testing and our third round of IVF, I continued to ask myself, *What is next if this doesn't work? What will the genetic testing tell us? Are we going to have embryos to freeze for another round of treatment? Are we going to adopt? Should we start looking into fostering children in need?* Questions flooded my mind, but I was not ready to give up.

Bryan and I were back in the tiny room where that first shocking conversation about our unexplained infertility occurred. "The worst kind of infertility," the doctor had said. But with the continued advancements of genetic testing, we hoped for some explanation. As we sat in the small, sterile room that smelled of latex gloves with familiar diagrams of women's uteruses on the wall, it occurred to me these results may not be what we were hoping for.

As the doctor walked into the room, I eyed the folder in her hands. It contained the genetic testing results of our embryos. Those results were our future. This felt eerily similar to sitting down at Creighton University to receive my BRCA1 genetic testing results. The doctor began to speak slowly just had Dr. Lynch had done 20 years prior, also while holding the results of my future in a plain manila folder.

"Bryan and Kathryn, I know this has been a long road for you, but I do not want you to lose hope."

I should have stopped her right there. My palms were sweaty as I clung to hope with all my might.

"The majority of your embryos are chromosomally abnormal."

"What does that mean?" Not being in the medical field, I didn't even know what the word chromosome meant. "And, what do you mean, abnormal?"

She gave us a brief 60-second science class on the spot, most of which I still did not understand. What I took from the conversation was that our embryos did not have all of the chromosomes required to implant into my uterus and eventually become a tiny little human, the tiny little human I was hoping to be holding in my arms someday.

I started to feel lightheaded. *What did all of this mean in regard to our future family? And what role did my genetics or Bryan's genetics play in this?* I silently questioned.

PGD testing was done on our ten embryos—nine were abnormal, one was normal. My throat began to tighten, and I knew once the tears began, they would not stop. Both the doctor and Bryan chose to look at our one "normal" embryo as a good thing.

This infertility journey had now been going on for four years, resulting in no children, not even a pregnancy. I was well over 30 years old and the chances of IVF working with two normal embryos was 50%. We only had one. This put our chances at 25%. I could have walked out that door and said enough was enough, but even though I was still scared and still cautious, I did believe.

We transferred the "normal" embryo, which we had also learned through genetic testing was a girl.

After an IVF transfer, it takes two weeks before a woman finds out if it works or not. Those two weeks are arduous. The day I was to receive the phone call regarding the potential little girl growing in my belly, I chose to stay home from work. I had spent too many hours trying to hide my crying in an office full of men who did not understand my situation. I decided to go to the gym to pass the time. As I was leaving the gym my phone rang. I immediately stopped in front of the bustling cafe of bodybuilders and protein shakes and cautiously answered.

The first words I heard were, "I am sorry."

Our third round of IVF had failed. I sat down on a bench with my phone in my hand and stared at it. My heart shattered into a million little pieces. Knowing it was a little girl was nearly unbearable. I had pictured a little girl with soft pigtails, a twirly dress, and her mama's heels. In this extreme brokenness, I also experienced numbness, as if my body was still there but with me removed from it, as if I were watching this young woman sitting on a bench near a cafe with no trace of emotion on her face, yet her face said so much. I had lost the ability to grieve or shed any more tears. The tear well had run dry.

I am not sure how long I sat on that bench. I drove home in silence. I did not call Bryan or my mom or my sisters. Telling them was almost harder than hearing it myself. In my mind, I was letting them down. They had all been riding this terrible roller coaster of infertility with me. We all wanted it to end.

Opting Out of Nipples
Bridget

In the summer of 2006, I went under the knife again, this time for the exchange surgery. It was such an easy surgery compared to what the mastectomy entailed. I was so excited to have *my* breasts put in and the hard expanders pulled out. My surgeon did a beautiful job; he even twisted up the skin for nipples and sutured them in place.

Some women choose to leave their nipples intact in a nipple sparing mastectomy. This is a choice that is up to each individual woman. However, there is still some breast tissue in the nipples, therefore it could be a source where cancer could develop. After everything I had been through, I wasn't going to be taken down by my nipples! So I opted out of a nipple-sparing mastectomy.

Out of all the things there are to "opt out of" in life, I never imagined nipples would be one of them. Life is funny like that. I had opted out of running in high school when I switched to cheerleading, but coming from a family of runners, it was an unavoidable fate. After many years of denying that running was part of my genetics, I finally accepted that I could be a runner too. My sisters and I began to run together; we ran many races together and have even run a few marathons. I've always enjoyed my sisters' company but running has bonded us on a whole new level.

One race morning prior to my exchange surgery, a particularly chilly fall day, we stood in our corrals waiting for the race to start. I hate this part of racing the most. Packed in like sardines with all the other (smelly) runners, anticipating the long run and journey ahead is torture, in my opinion. Kathryn, Maureen, and I often try to distract one another from our misery by joking around and trying to guess who is responsible for the bad body odor or righteous fart that just escaped a fellow runner.

This race day was no exception to our pre-race antics. As

the biting wind swept through the runners Kathryn uncomfortably stated, "Gosh, it's so cold my nipples could poke someone's eyes out right now."

Maureen and I giggled furiously.

Maureen then said, "I guess that's what's nice about your mastectomy, Bridget. No more nipples!"

I laughed. "You're right! I got to opt out of nipples!"

Kathryn and Maureen shouted in almost unison, "That's it! That's the name of our book. Nipples Optional!"

The three of us cheered at our cleaver epiphany. Then with a whip-like crack, the race gun went off and the three of us started the race, laughing and elated we had our book title.

Opting out of nipples gave me the chance to get the tattoos I never did as a rebellious college student. I chose to have 3-D nipples tattooed on instead. This was the last step to complete my breast previvor journey. Tattooing 3-D nipples is a way to present the illusion of nipples. Some breast surgeon clinics now even employ nurse tattoo artists on staff. It is a wonderful way that a woman can feel halfway normal after having her breasts removed. When my two best girlfriends got butterflies on their lower backs at age 18, I chickened out. Which is odd because I was always up for anything defiant. Now I had another chance, and I took it. This would be my first tattoo(s). I was so excited!

My doctor's office did not offer nipple tattooing, so I went to Downtown Kansas City to see a man named Whispering Danny. He resided in a typical tattoo parlor—small, dirty, with the heavy stench of nicotine wafting through the air. Despite the atmosphere of the tattoo parlor, the tattooist came highly recommended by my breast surgeon. Whispering Danny had lost his grandmother to breast cancer and he donated half his nipple tattooing proceeds to support breast cancer organizations.

On my first visit to the tattoo parlor, I was sent home because my scars hadn't healed enough. I was grateful for the tattooist's honesty, but I felt desperate to have my chest look somewhat "normal" again.

The second time I visited Whispering Danny for my nipple tattoos was before my wedding in 2009. I thought it'd be fun to surprise my husband-to-be. Whispering Danny again turned me away. We were headed to Dominican Republic on our honeymoon and would be getting in the ocean. A new tattoo is similar to a fresh scar and should not be exposed to any potential infectors such as bacteria in the ocean water.

I must have been deterred because I waited many years to visit Whispering Danny for a third time. This time I was good to go. Third time's a charm. I invited my sisters and mother to join me for the special occasion.

So in 2015, I reclined in Whispering Danny's tattoo chair as my breasts, or what was left of them, hung out. Whispering Danny first inspected my chest closely. He analyzed the "nipples" that my plastic surgeon had made for me during my exchange surgery.

Danny let out a heavy sigh of annoyance. "You're not going to want to hear this, Bridget."

Oh no, I thought, *please no more bad news.*

"The nipples your doctor made for you are not symmetrical. I am going to have to tattoo your nipples in a different place than he placed your nipples."

"Oh, Danny! If you think this is going to bother me after everything I've been through, I am going to make this real easy. I don't care! Do what you need to do."

A giant smile erupted across his face. I had just given an artist permission to be as creative as he wanted to be.

Next decision: the nipple color. He mixed up a few shades of pink to create a nipple color of my liking. We decided on a delicate shade of pink. If someone had told me that one day I'd be choosing a nipple color for myself, I would have found that very hard to believe, and laughable. But the intricacies of nipple tattooing are vast and the complexities of being BRCA positive are endless. I accepted it all as I was just happy to have those cancer time bombs off my chest.

After he marked the proper areas for my nipples, we got started. Danny approached me with what can only be described as a tool resembling a dental drill. He placed the needle on my chest and began to drill. With no prior experience with tattooing, I hadn't considered it would be painful. Plus, I had expected my skin to be numb from the nerve damage caused by the mastectomy. But those tattoos hurt like a son of a gun. I have no idea why people willingly subject themselves repeatedly to voluntary tattoo pain.

I gripped the sides of Danny's worn leather chair and clenched my teeth through the entire process.

This better be worth it! I thought to myself.

My new tattoos took quite some time, the better part of an hour. Danny put his final touches on my chest and handed me a mirror. As I held up the mirror in front of my body, tears welled up in my eyes. My breasts appeared normal for the first time in a long time. He gave me back a piece of myself I didn't know was missing.

I was relieved to have had the surgery behind me (and the tattoos, thank God), but I still had a big job to do. My little sister Maureen was just at the beginning of her BRCA1 journey, and I needed to show her there was nothing to fear.

Maureen and I are a lot alike. We think, look, and act so much alike that even though Maureen is three years younger than me, we are oftentimes mistaken for twins. And we both suffer from anxiety. Maureen and I spend many conversations talking each other off ledges that don't exist. I'm sure we coined the phrase "anticipatory anxiety" long before Dr. Phil did. Many of our anxieties are health related, undeniably related to the fact we are so acutely aware of our cancer risks. If one of us is panicking, the conversation almost always starts with, "Calm down and get off Google."

As Maureen recovered from her double mastectomy, I knew her genetic status had the ability to throw her into a full-blown anxiety meltdown. It was up to me to demonstrate to her that life would be normal—even better—after surgery. Post mastectomy, I finished nursing school, I ran marathons, I dated (a lot), I even did jumping jacks in front of her to show her my full range of motion. But in the end, Maureen needed to experience it herself to fully understand. Still, I would be there with her every step of the way.

God and Xanax
Maureen

When my turn came to decide about nipple-sparing surgery, I opted out, same as Bridget. This was an easy decision. I couldn't imagine going through a procedure as extensive as a double mastectomy then still getting breast cancer because of the breast tissue left behind in teeny tiny nipples.

Also, I told myself, if I didn't have nipples, I wouldn't have to wear a strapless bra when I wore cute tops (Bear in mind, I was only 23 years old.) Problem solved.

I have on occasion considered nipple tattoos. However, I went with Bridget when she got her nipples tattooed on and that was enough for me. It's not the pain I'm worried about. It's the needle so close to my implants that scares me. I know the needle won't puncture my implant. I know it won't. I know I have muscle between my skin and implant. *But,* I just can't help but wonder, *what if it did?* And for that reason, I remain nippleless. For now, at least.

I would like to get a tattoo someday. I also want nipples. I have toyed with the idea of a tattoo of nipples, just not on my breasts. They would be tasteful, of course.

When I told Josh about my idea, he laughed nervously. I couldn't tell if he was laughing because he was afraid I would actually do it or if he thought I was joking. I guess I don't know either.

If I am being honest with myself, I think it was easy to opt out of nipples, and breasts, because I had emotionally distanced myself from them. I knew from a young age not to get attached. So when it came time, physically distancing myself wasn't so hard.

I didn't resent my breasts in any way. In fact, I liked them, a lot. Some days I actually miss them. But then one of my sisters reminds me that they wouldn't be now what they once were. Not after three babies. However, I knew from the time they came in when I was 13 ½ that they wouldn't be around for long.

And so I prepared early to say goodbye for good.

I was fortunate to recover from my mastectomy in the comfort of my parents' home. My support and nursing staff (Bridget and my mom) took very good care of me, which is more than I can say about the hospital staff. While I was being discharged from the hospital following my surgery, I quickly grew frustrated with the lack of information I was provided. The nurse must have noticed and tried to justify the rushed discharge by saying, "Your mom is a nurse, you will be fine."

A baby nurse. My mom is a BABY nurse! Babies don't have breasts, you idiot! I screamed in my head. I digress.

Many people sent cards and flowers, praying for a quick recovery. My future mother-in-law, Mary, offered to bring me lunch. I'd been cooped up in the house for several days and was eager to enjoy the nice fall weather, so I recommended we go out for lunch instead. I'm sure it was not her preference to go to lunch at Panera with her future daughter-in-law with drainage tubes pinned to her sweater, but she kindly agreed.

A few days into my recovery, it was time to have my drainage tubes removed. I'm not sure if this was supposed to be done by a real nurse or my personal nursing staff, but ultimately my mother did it. Not being accustomed to "at home care" like this, I was understandably very anxious. While my mom investigated my incisions, Bridget held me down and forced a Xanax in my mouth. It wasn't a pretty scene, but it was done in a loving manner (which is more than I can say for the hospital staff).

During my recovery, I also received a thoughtful bouquet of flowers and a note from my college roommate, Alisha. Her note read, "You cannot direct the wind, but you can adjust the sails." There were no truer words to describe this shitty situation. And life, as well. Life is a series of adjusting the sails over and over again, just hoping you don't capsize the boat.

The remainder of my recovery was uneventful, for me at least. For Josh, it was another story. One day, in particular, was a little more awkward than others. There we were, just me, my mom and Josh, sitting in the bathroom, looking at my drainage tube scars located on the side of my implants, trying to figure out what the black "string" hanging out of it was. Was it a stitch? Was it dried blood? No one could quite figure it out. Fortunately, I was under a considerable amount of drugs still and didn't feel too awkward. Josh, on the other hand, must have felt more than a little uncomfortable staring at his future wife's reconstructed breast bumps, sans nipples, alongside his future mother-in-law. *Poor, poor Josh.* Thank God, it was just a string of dried blood left over from my drainage tubes and we were all able to move on and forget about it. Everyone except Josh, maybe.

In all seriousness, learning my genetic results and undergoing a prophylactic double mastectomy did cause me to question God. I occasionally found myself asking God, "Why?" Why couldn't I live a "normal" 20-something-year-old life? Why did God give me this gene? Why did I have to worry about cancer stealing my life at a young age? Why does He let bad things happen? I have never questioned the existence of God, but I do have some lingering questions about how and why things happen the way they do.

I was born, raised, and continue to be a practicing Catholic. As a child, we attended Mass on a weekly basis as a family, and occasionally volunteered at the soup kitchen with our church. These are important traditions that I hope to continue with my children.

Yes, I chose to attend Creighton, a Jesuit university, but not because of the religious aspect. Something just felt right about Creighton. I am a fairly intuitive person and there is no doubt in my mind that Creighton is where I was meant to be. I enjoyed the service aspect of the school and loved going to Sunday evening candlelight Mass with friends. It created a strong community that I still miss to this day. And, for the first time in my life, being Catholic was cool.

Attending Creighton didn't revive my Catholic roots, but meeting Josh at Creighton did. Josh was also raised Catholic, but unlike me, he was a good Catholic. Because of Josh, I started attending Mass again. We both wanted to raise our children Catholic, the same way we were, and this began with a traditional Catholic wedding.

We were getting ready for our very Catholic wedding when my anxiety hit. As I sat in the bridal room while guests started to arrive, my sisters offered to help me climb out of the small bathroom window. I declined. This had nothing to do with Josh. I loved Josh. This had to do with my fear of fainting at the altar, and maybe something to do with making one of the biggest decisions of my life. I said a prayer in the back of the church that day to calm my anxious heart. God must have been watching over me that day, because I made it down the aisle to marry Josh. (God, or the Xanax. Not sure which one kicked in first).

I didn't know at the time that my battle with anxiety had just begun.

PART V: EMBRACING THE UNKNOWN

Sometimes it might surprise you.

Walking Down an Unknown Road Together
Kathryn

Bryan and I agreed to put everything behind us and start the next year as our "adoption year." Since our procreation year(s) went down in a ball of flames, and IVF had repeatedly failed, it was time to start a new adventure. But this mountain, the "Adoption Adventure" that we set out to climb, was much more difficult than we had ever imagined.

Right off the bat I started firing questions at Bryan. Open, closed? Domestic, international? An older child? A newborn baby? The big-headed determination that had gotten me this far was stronger than ever.

Bryan on the other hand was tired of all of it. It paralyzed him to even think about it, thus causing him to shut down. And I don't blame him. Fertility treatments had been daunting, adoption even more so. I pleaded with him to engage in this adventure with me instead of being a bystander in it.

"Don't lose me now, Bryan. I am just getting started."

In true businesswoman fashion, I put together a fancy PowerPoint presentation and presented our options to him. I included columns for us to make a pros and cons list.

For example, adopting a child from overseas—
Pro: you get to travel overseas
Con: you have to travel overseas.
Adopting an older child—
Pro: you get an older child.
Con: you now have an older child.

We were getting nowhere. This was not as easy as putting your name on a list and being called in the middle of the night to pick up a new little baby.

Truthfully neither of us could wrap our heads around having a child who was not biologically ours. Genetics allow a person to paint a picture of what life would look like when you combine two people. In the course of trying to start a family, I had always pictured a little boy who looked like Bryan.

Long legs, greenish eyes, and tawny colored skin. I knew my boy would be as determined as Bryan but as kind as his mama. I pictured a little girl who had light brown hair, brown eyes, and tiny little ears. And I knew my little girl would take on my love of running and stun the world with her calculating personality. The mental image I had designed of these little people was tough to erase.

We knew we could love any little baby who came into our life but if we are being honest, we were scared. Too many "what ifs" to consider. What if we didn't bond with the baby? What if the baby didn't bond with us? And so we moved forward very, very slowly, taking baby steps (no pun intended).

We began by meeting with an adoption agency. They suggested we send out a Christmas card announcing we were about to embark on the journey of adoption. I thought it sounded a little vain, but isn't that what Christmas cards are for? To tell everyone all of the amazing things happening in your life? Or less than amazing things in our case. In a nutshell, our 2011 Christmas card said, "Merry Christmas. Can't get pregnant. If you know anyone who wants to give us a baby, here is our email address." *God, there are so many things wrong with that sentence.*

We learned in our adoption classes that birth mothers do not "give up" babies, they "place them" for adoption. We also learned that it is probably a good idea to remember the password to the newly created email account set up specifically for adoption if you ever want to read any emails people may have sent you. (P.S. If you're reading this and sent us an email, I am sorry I did not respond. But, if you still have a baby, we would gladly accept him or her.)

If you had told me within nine months of sending that card, we would be holding our newborn baby, I would have laughed at you.

On a bright and cold Sunday morning in March 2012 (three months after we sent the questionable Christmas card), Bryan picked up his phone to listen to his voicemail as we were pulling out of the church parking lot. A familiar voice began,

"Bryan, this is a strange voicemail to be leaving you, but..." and so our adoption journey began.

Bryan's friend said she knew someone who knew someone who was looking at placing her baby up for adoption and to give her a call back and she would give us the details. We called back and got her voicemail. *Could she not have answered the phone?* Bryan and I tried to move on with our daily activities and decided to run a few errands.

We were in Costco, standing next to discounted wrapping paper, when our friend finally called us back. Bryan guardedly spoke to her as I paced the aisle watching his face. I made a few hand motions, waving in the aisle, that said, "Give me something, anything!"

Bryan finally hung up the phone. I demanded the details. The only thing he was able to give me was *another* person's phone number with instructions to "Text this other lady and ask her but don't call her because she has three kids and is very busy."

That was it, I had to take over. Men are clearly not into details, even when it pertains to the single most important phone call of your life. I quickly pulled out my phone and texted this other person who ended up being the birth mother's mom's friend, Jen.

I also called my sisters after Bryan and I specifically discussed not telling anyone. We didn't want anyone else on this roller coaster with us. Well, he didn't want anyone, but I wanted my sisters. I *needed* my sisters. They could offer the love of sisters and the support of best friends. I was able to get ahold of Maureen first.

"I have to tell you something," I spit out the second she answered the phone.

Maureen is clever and witty. By far, much smarter than I am. She has always been a strong woman who is very much in charge of her own destiny. Maureen is also funny, a sense of humor I would pay money for.

"You're pregnant?" she questioned, knowing very well

that ship had sailed.

"God, no." I laughed. "But we are going to have a baby."

"Did one of your friends offer to give you an egg so you could get pregnant?"

This was a valid question. One of our friends actually did offer to do this for us. A true act of friendship but unfortunately one that did not work out.

I went on to explain to Maureen what had transpired since we had left church that morning. She launched into a million questions. Questions I didn't have any answers to or had not even considered. Maureen's business sense and approach to life is one to be admired. She had asked similar questions when she was debating on having her mastectomy after finding out she was BRCA1 positive. I would have just had the mastectomy, but she likes to look at all the angles of a problem. She counseled me on questions I should ask and think through before moving forward. Maureen is six years younger than me but, in many ways, wiser.

It wasn't until the next day when I heard back from Jen. It was a cold, dark gloomy March day, with a late season snowstorm approaching. I sat in my office, wearing a black pencil skirt, a light blue collared shirt, nude heels, and tortoise colored glasses. I was proud of my distinct, professional look. As I stared out the window at the approaching snowstorm, I thought about what possibly lay ahead of us. I was jolted out of my daydream when the phone rang. I jumped, grabbed the phone, bobbled it a few times and finally blurted, "This is Kathryn."

"Are you ready to be a mama?! It's a boy! These things move very fast so you need an attorney!" exclaimed the woman on the other end of the line. I learned that the mother of the teenager who was pregnant did not want any involvement, which is why she enlisted her best friend, Jen, to support her daughter. They referred to her as Aunt Jen.

I paced the office, my heart jumping, as I listened to Jen share scattered details. In an instant, everything I had worked so hard for was coming to fruition.

I collected myself and called Bryan. "Answer the phone, please answer the phone," I whispered.

"Hey babe."

"She called me back."

"Who called you back?"

"The lady. The lady from yesterday. About the adoption." I said, mildly irritated. Clearly this had not been consuming Bryan's mind as much as mine.

"Oh, ok. What did she say?" he replied nonchalantly.

"It's a boy and we need an attorney." My voice turned giddy with excitement.

"Excuse me, what? I don't understand."

"The adoption. The baby. It's ours." My excitement was beginning to fade with his lackluster responses.

"But... I thought we were just going to get information... I didn't realize we were actually going through with an adoption."

"Holy hell, Bryan. What is happening? We decided to do adoption." I was livid.

"Yes, but this is all moving too fast."

And at that, I hung up the phone.

Fast was how adoption worked in my mind. You get a call about a baby and you go after it.

I soon learned Bryan was just as emotionally invested in our adoption adventure as I was; he just didn't show it the same way I did. Bryan wanted to be a part of it all, and I needed to let him. I had been trying to command something that was completely out of my hands (similar to fertility treatments), and I was not letting him participate. Also, the phrase "You're going to be a dad. It's a boy. We need an attorney" is not something you call your husband with at work on a random Monday. The call should have started out, "Are you sitting down? I have some exciting news to share and we are going to do this together."

What Bryan (nor I) didn't realize at the time is that our adoption adventure was about to turn into a barrage of texts, phone calls, emotions, meetings, and lengthy conversations.

He Fits Me Like A Mitten
Bridget

Kathryn has been the model big sister of our family since we were all children. Maureen and I were her little ducklings. I believe if it were up to Kathryn, she would have chosen to make herself the BRCA mutation carrier and the rest of us negative. She was, however, struck by the infertility lightning bolt instead.

I know it was difficult for Kathryn to learn Maureen and I were BRCA1 carriers and then witness us endure major surgery. The three of us have a bond that is without judgment and full of love, empathy, and endless laughter.

To watch a selfless, mothering, nurturing, successful, kind, and loving person be deprived the opportunity to become a mother was so damn hard. Not only for her and Bryan, but for whatever child should have been theirs.

At one point, someone suggested to Kathryn that maybe she wasn't meant to be a mom. I know it is difficult for people to come up with the right thing to say to a person who is suffering, but this was definitely one of the worst. Kathryn was meant to be a mother and I knew this in the deepest part of my soul.

It also didn't help that the moment my husband looked at me, I was pregnant.

As much as I don't believe in fate or that one person is made for you, I do believe Ryan and I belong together. He fits me like a glove, as I do him. Actually, more like a mitten. We fit each other like a mitten—everyone needs a little wiggle room. Like Kathryn, Ryan is extremely selfless and kind. He smiles at strangers, waves at neighbors, and instantly strikes up conversations with just about anyone. I, on the other hand, was born with a resting bitch face. People are always telling me to smile. I think, *I am!* But, maybe I'm not.

Ryan was born and raised in Chicago. We met when Ryan came to Kansas City to visit his cousin who was dating my good friend. Despite his kindness and humor, I deemed him geographically undesirable. He worked in Chicago, and I was just about to start nursing school in Kansas. Yet somehow, I couldn't shake the charming, 27-year-old, aviation-degreed Chicagoan from my mind.

We attempted a long-distance relationship for a short while, until Ryan called a couple days before his next visit and cancelled. Ryan explained that he just didn't see how a long-distance relationship could work between us. I understood, but I was hurt and devastated.

The good thing about Ryan ending our relationship was that I didn't have to reveal to him that I was about to have my breasts removed that coming winter. I had been trying to figure out how to tell him.

"Hey, you like me now? How about with no breasts?"

Isn't that enticing for a 27-year-old man?

Ryan's cousin got wind of Ryan ending our relationship and was furious with Ryan. He thought Ryan had ended it because of my "situation," so he called Ryan to yell at him for what he had done. But Ryan knew nothing about my being a BRCA1 carrier or my impending double mastectomy.

After my mastectomy that winter, I received an anonymous bouquet of Gerbera daisies. My mom and I were in the kitchen excitedly talking about who they could have been from. I even called the flower company, but they would not reveal the customer. I had an inkling who they were from, so I sent a simple email to Ryan.

"How did you know Gerbera daisies were my favorite?"

And, with his simple, kind gesture, we started to talk again. Before long Ryan relocated to Kansas City and soon after we were married.

If Ryan hadn't sent the daisies, I'm not sure we would have reconnected. I am pretty sure he'd be a stock trader living in the Chicago suburbs married to a Karen, with 2.5 kids, a cat, and white picket fence. I can't really say where I would be. One of two places: either living in the suburbs of Kansas, married with a buttload of kids and three dogs; or residing on an island in the

Caribbean, braiding tourists' hair during the day and bartending at night. But I digress.

Ryan fit into our family like a puzzle piece. He was extremely understanding of my decision to have preventative surgery and probably quite relieved that I chose to do so. Watching his own father lose his life to cancer had been earth-shattering for Ryan. I'm sure he would have forfeited much more than a wife with natural breasts to avoid her suffering from the same beast.

Ryan and I hadn't even been married a year when we decided to try for a baby. I had worried about my own ability to conceive because of what I had seen Kathryn go through. Our attempt to conceive started as a sort of an experiment. Cautious to expect too much, we said to each other, "Let's just see how this goes..."

The Weight of Knowing
Maureen

Not long after my prophylactic mastectomy, our younger cousin Kate emailed us. It was her turn to find out her results and she was seeking our support. This is her email:

Hello ladies,
I recently got tested for the BRCA1 mutation. I know you all did and I'm curious to see If maybe you have advice for the waiting process. I didn't think I would find it emotional. This is some-thing I knew I would need to deal with as I'm sure all of you did as well, but I'm finding it harder than expected. I am trying to look at it positively. Was this difficult for you? I find many people don't know what this is and it's hard to get people to understand. Anyway, I am just trying to reach out. I know we aren't that close, but anything you feel comfortable sharing, I would appreciate. I look up to all of you. You are all strong, suc-cessful women.
Thank you!
Love, Kate

It was my turn to provide guidance and help Katie as she too processed receiving genetic test results. I thought of a few things that helped me through my experience and sent her the following email:

Dear Katie,
One of the most important things to remember is that getting tested for the BRCA gene mutation is a blessing! It may not seem like it now, or the day you find out your results, but we are far more fortunate than the Hare women who came before us. We have the opportunity to control something that, for them, was very uncontrollable.
For me, it was very helpful to keep a journal of my experience. It

helps to write down how you are feeling and how others react. Some experiences are sad to go back and read, although others are very comforting. I love going back to read how my college roommates responded to the news (with incredible support), to laugh at the stupid things my doctors have said to me, to remember the people who were at my surgery when I woke up.

I have also found that a strong support system of women has been incredibly helpful. I remember Bridget doing jumping jacks in front of me the day after my surgery to prove to me that I would regain full mobility of my arms (which I eventually did). I don't know if it was the painkillers or seeing her doing jumping jacks, but it made me laugh when I was very down. So, feel free to call or email any of us! We have been there and love sharing our BRCA1 stories. Also, your mom and aunts have all been through it, too. Although it is a little sad, we all have this common bond and are here to support each other.

Lastly, if you have the BRCA1 mutation, remember that it's not a death sentence. It is truly a blessing to have as much knowledge and control as we do. My doctor told me that your odds of developing cancer drop from roughly 90% to hopefully 1% after a mastectomy. I find this very comforting! Those are better odds than the average woman without the gene.

Whether or not we have the gene, it is part of who we are. Other great genes come from Hare women that I would never give up, even if I could, to replace the BRCA1 gene.

Love, Maureen

What I wanted to express to Kate was that finding out you are BRCA1 positive can have such an incredible impact on your future and your identity, but perhaps not in the way you might expect. Receiving your genetic results, whether positive or negative, compels individuals to evaluate themselves, who they are, and who they want to become.

For me, learning I was positive determined a lot for my future. Immediately, I knew that I wanted a family and that meant having children very young. That also meant getting married young. So, I married Josh, had three babies and settled down close to my family. Would I have made those decisions if I wasn't BRCA positive? Honestly, I don't know. I'll never know. If I was BRCA1 negative would I have followed my free-spirited study abroad boyfriend to New York City and still be living in a 600-square-foot bedroom without kids when I was 35? Again, I don't know. Regardless, bearing the weight of knowing my genetic status made me look deep within myself to examine what I wanted. It helped me understand who I was, both as a BRCA gene carrier and as a typical 20-something female. I had to decide what I wanted my future to look like.

Being BRCA positive had become part of my identity. The strong psychological impact is not easy to overlook. The BRCA identity goes much deeper than just an aspect of my DNA that doesn't appropriately suppress tumors. It defined how I saw and treated the world around me. Personally, receiving my genetic results, having a prophylactic mastectomy, and becoming a previvor made me feel strong, brave, and optimistic.

Years after my mastectomy, however, I received news that shook my BRCA identity to the core and made me question all of those decisions I had so confidently made.

The Universe Knew
Kathryn

Over the next few days, the pregnant teen changed her mind (more than once) about placing her baby, then requested photos and personal information about Bryan and me and debated whether or not she wanted to meet us. Our family's future lay in the hands of a 15-year-old pregnant teenager.

While this was all happening—and for some inexplicable reason (maybe it was the 50% discount... *a.k.a. red flag*)—we decided to proceed with a fourth round of IVF. Following this egg retrieval process, I checked myself into the ER due to (yet again) more complications from the IVF. I thought I was experiencing ovarian hyperstimulation—a dangerous, exaggerated response to the ovaries being stimulated by hormones to produce eggs. (Turns out, I didn't have ovarian hyperstimulation, just constipation. Infertility treatments can really humble a young woman.)

I was lying in the hospital bed when my phone rang.

When I answered, Jen talked quickly about how much they wanted to meet us. I hung on every word. As she launched into the story about how this baby came to be, my IV drip began to sing out an ear-piercing beeping sound. The nurse rushed in to check on it, but I quickly shooed her away, intent on arranging a meeting with the birth mom and her family.

Coincidentally, the meeting was on the same day I had the embryos (from the fourth round of IVF) transferred back into me. I was supposed to be on bedrest for three days.

My heart was not into IVF this fourth time around. It had failed me too many times and at this point I was just going through the motions. I was also irritated with my fertility doctor. Not because none of my treatments were successful but because when I asked her about additional testing, she told me there were no other options for me. I didn't believe that, but I also didn't know where else to turn. I wanted to trust her; however, she had already categorized me as your typical woman who couldn't possibly get pregnant but was still determined that if she tried enough times, it might work. Well, as my mom said at one point, "Even a blind squirrel can find a nut." I refused to lose hope.

All the fertility specialist could offer me was a fourth round of IVF at a 50% discount. I felt helpless, hopeless, and also pissed. But, regrettably, I was not brave enough to challenge her.

Waiting to meet our potential birth mother was arguably harder than waiting to find out if IVF worked or not. At any point our phone could ring to inform us of her decision to cancel. While the IVF process challenged me physically, no one could have prepared me for how the adoption process challenged me mentally.

The meeting day finally arrived. The reluctant birth mother and her overexcited "Aunt Jen" showed up at our house right on time. Bryan answered the door, forbidding me to move from the couch (due to my bed rest). In walked this adorably pregnant, blonde haired, blue-eyed girl. Clearly, this was not a comfortable situation for her, and I bet my right arm she would rather have been anywhere else than at my house. I, on the other hand, was thrilled beyond belief and filled with hope.

The conversation felt somewhat forced. Everyone stared at the four beautifully decorated cupcakes in the middle of the table but didn't touch them. I spent the entire visit wondering what she thought of us. *Do we look okay? How is my hair? Did we say the right things? Does she like our house? Is it too big? Too small?* I began to spiral downward in my head. The situation was all very intense. And if this was too much for me, a 34-year-old woman, how does a 15-year-old girl feel? She showed very little emotion and even less eye contact.

We did, however, learn that she was 20 weeks along. Halfway there. *We could be parents in 20 short weeks!* She left the short meeting without any hint whether we would hear from her again.

That night Bryan and I lay on our closet floor talking about what we would do if IVF worked and she asked us to be the adoptive parents. Would we take both babies? Would she still ask us to be the adoptive parents if we became pregnant?

Well, I guess the universe knew how to solve our problem because we found out shortly after that fateful meeting with our potential birth mother that IVF did not work. Again.

Four rounds of IVF and we were done. Thank God. The drugs, the money, the emotions, the doctor appointments—all had hijacked so many years of our life. I felt like I had been removed from my life for six years and then finally brought back. I felt liberated knowing we were done. And, although we came up empty handed, we were at peace with it. It's easy to be at peace with something when you have something else in your back pocket.

So, ahead we went with our fingers, toes, and all limbs crossed that she would choose us.

I desperately wanted to tell our parents about the potential adoption. I desired our announcement to be special, the same way people get to experience when they announce their pregnancy to the world. But we also didn't want to say anything until we knew for sure where this adoption was going. I settled for casually mentioning the potential adoption to my family over dinner. And I told them, "Hope for the best but expect the worst."

The Hardest Words I've Ever Had to Say
Bridget

Despite my grave concern over my own ability to become pregnant, I became pregnant very quickly, like, shockingly quick. I took a pregnancy test while Ryan worked in the garage one evening. It took about three seconds for the "pregnant" to pop up on the digital screen. My first thought was, *Where is the 'not'?* My second thought was of Kathryn, followed by tears because I was pregnant instead of her.

In fact, when I first told my parents I was pregnant, they were elated, but their happiness quickly subsided as they asked how I was going to tell Kathryn. I hadn't a clue how I was going to tell my infertile sister that I was apparently super fucking fertile. I felt so guilty. How could I have done this to her? She is one of the people I love most in the world and I felt like I had betrayed her in some way.

I finally mustered up the courage to tell Kathryn. I asked her to go on a walk with me one afternoon. She probably thought this was weird. We never went on walks together. We ran. We were, after all, runners. But I wasn't about to go on a run and jumble up the tiny baby growing delicately inside of me.

On a cloudy spring day, we strolled down the sidewalk in her beautiful suburban neighborhood. My heart raced. I didn't know how I was going to say the words that were going to break her heart. Finally, I just blurted it out.

"I'm pregnant. I am so sorry, Kathryn, but I am pregnant."

She stopped, turned, and looked at me.

"Oh my God, you are?" Her eyebrows went up and she smiled, big. "Bridget, that is amazing!"

She was, of course, extremely supportive and genuinely happy for me. The next day she came over with a stack of baby and pregnancy books. That is Kathryn.

Deep down for her though, I knew it stung. It stung for me too. I did not want to be the source of any additional hurt to my sister, and I didn't really even want to celebrate my pregnancy.

I was very happy to be starting a family, but I wanted so badly for it to be her. I even started having some absurd thoughts. I started to wish something bad would happen to me during my pregnancy. Not something too bad, nothing to affect the baby, just something bad enough to even the heartbreak score between us. Instead, my pregnancy was flawless.

We chose not to find out the gender of the baby during the pregnancy, as I think it is one of the only wonderful surprises left in life. Ryan, though, thought he saw a penis on our twenty-week ultrasound and declared I was carrying a healthy baby boy. I had a strong feeling I was carrying a girl, but I didn't share this with anyone. I mean, poor Ryan was practically shouting from the rooftops that he had spawned a male.

Having a daughter would be bittersweet because it would mean that, if she carried the BRCA mutation, she would be facing a future either riddled with worry over a cancer diagnosis or filled with surgeries. Did I want my child to have to face that?

When I was young—pre-prophylactic double mastectomy and Whispering Danny's tattoos—I always thought I wanted to deliver my babies naturally. To prove I was a real woman. To hell with that. I had nothing left to prove. Bring on the drugs and an induction. I chose to schedule an induction on the baby's due date.

My entire family came to the hospital for the birth. I wanted to share bringing our baby into this world with all of the people I love. During early labor everyone hung out in the hospital room with me. My sisters braided my hair, Ryan videoed with our brand new camera, my mother-in-law watched the baby's heartbeat and my contractions on the monitor, my brother-in-law read the newspaper in the corner, my brother and his wife, Amanda, shared a chair and chatted excitedly, and my mom paced at the foot of my bed waiting for her first grandbaby's arrival. Only in my family.

I am not completely deranged, though. I did kick the boys out—except for Ryan—when it came time to start pushing. My sisters stated they would stay at the "head of the bed." However, there really is no "head of the bed" in a delivery. It's all out there for everyone to see. Somehow Maureen got handed the video camera to document the whole thing. I laugh because I am sure her first reaction was, "No, but thanks." Nonetheless, she agreed, and I treasure the sound of her sobbing as she taped the birth.

As our baby emerged, the doctor's hand covered the baby's bottom so no one could see the gender, but I caught a sneak peek and thought, *Oh my God, it is a girl.*

Of course, a couple seconds later my mother shouted, "WE DON'T KNOW WHAT IT IS! WHAT IS IT?"

Everyone cried and cheered when the doctor prompted Ryan to announce it was a girl. But I saw it first. I saw her first. Our baby, Penelope Kathryn, was born on December 16, 2010.

Ryan will be a source of strength for Penelope should she one day discover she is a BRCA1 carrier. She will have him and a family to be her pillar of strength if the time comes when she has to make difficult decisions about the future of her body and the future of her health. Despite what her DNA may be—that is still unknown—she is lucky. I am lucky. We are lucky.

My Little Loves
Maureen

Life is hard. I often joke that life is downhill after day one. I know that's a very pessimistic thing to say, especially for a semi-optimistic person. It's not that I think life gets worse, necessarily, but I do believe it gets a whole lot harder. Maybe my downhill philosophy is a result of prophylactic mastectomy at age 23, just maybe. Or maybe that was just the beginning of a life filled with the unexpected.

What makes life beautiful is the unconditional love that my family, friends, and pets (yes, pets) provide. My family especially has been such a positive influence in my life. They have shaped the person I am today (them, and my breast surgeon who shaped me into a much more voluptuous woman than I wanted to be).

Although we Winns share almost everything as a family, including the BRCA1 gene, when it came to childbearing, I didn't necessarily think this was something we needed to do together. I was wrong.

I'll admit, when Penelope was born, I wasn't super keen on watching Bridget push an eight-pound baby out of her you-know-what. Is there no mystery left in the world? Call me old fashioned, but I was perfectly happy sitting in the waiting room with the men. Instead, I got the whole show of Penelope's birth. It is still a picture I can't get out of my mind (as hard as I try), and for that I am eternally grateful. Because it was hands down the most beautiful sight I have seen in my entire life. We laughed, we cried. It was one of those candid and emotional moments that are so rare and beautiful they instantly teach you the meaning of life.

During this same time, Kathryn continued her wait for a tiny life of her own. I was working the day she expected to find out the results of their latest round of IVF and was anxiously awaiting her phone call. When my phone rang, I stepped out of my cubicle to take the call and instantly knew it wasn't the news I was hoping for. Another round had failed. However, Kathryn went on, "But, there is a little baby…"

I paced up and down the hallway in my office with tears in my eyes as she told me about the teen mother and their soon-to-be child. The details weren't finalized but I knew deep down in my heart this was going to be their baby. How long we (Kathryn and Bryan and the rest of us) had all waited!

Soon, it was my turn to give it a go. When Josh and I discussed starting a family I feared that, like Kathryn, I would not be able to get pregnant. The fear of infertility weighed on my mind constantly. Consequently, I was anxious to start trying, doubtful it would happen quickly, if at all.

One day, I blurted to Josh, "We should try to get pregnant."

"But our European Procreation Vacation isn't planned for another four months. Do you really want to be pregnant in Europe?"

"I won't be pregnant by then and even if by some chance I am, I won't care if I am pregnant in Europe."

Well, I was pregnant in Europe and I did care.

Although I was incredibly thankful to be pregnant, I was also incredibly sober at Oktoberfest in Munich, Germany. Thankfully, non-alcoholic German beer is better than most alcoholic American beer, so it all worked out.

Theodore Patrick came into the world with a bang on February 2, 2013. Well, not so much a bang, as a slight shove into my ureter causing my left kidney to dilate. While most babies tend to grow out, my little Groundhog Day baby tried to burrow in.

The morning the abdominal pain started, I called my doctor's nurse from work to see what they recommended I do. The nurse told me to take some Tylenol and lie down. I did. It didn't work. In fact, the pain continued to grow in intensity. Crying in excruciating pain, I called my mother.

My mother yelled, "You get to the hospital right now. You should never be in that much pain when you are pregnant!"

Twenty minutes later I lay in a hospital bed, still in pain, holding Josh's hand and fearing my placenta had abrupted. Thankfully, an ultrasound ruled out any abruption and showed a perfectly healthy baby. However, due to the pain, my doctor thoroughly discussed emergency C-section with my family (not with me, I was high on morphine). I am thankful my parents and husband were there to advocate for me when I was unable to advocate for myself.

Thirty minutes and one spinal block later, my sweet Teddy Bear arrived. I heard my baby's cry for the first time, the sweetest sound I had ever heard, and the pain was gone.

A few days later, I sat in Teddy's nursery, rocked him to sleep and I cried. I held in my hands everything I ever wanted. My life, for the first time, felt complete.

As I rocked Teddy, I snuggled him up to my chest and fed him a warm bottle. One of the unfortunate consequences of having a prophylactic mastectomy before bearing children is not being able to breastfeed. But I'll be honest, the idea of a newborn's life depending on my breasts' ability to produce milk, and my little tot eventually chewing on my poor nipples when his or her teeth finally came in, had always sounded absolutely awful to me. However, as a lactation consultant, my mother pounded in the importance of breast milk. Because she deemed breast milk so incredibly beneficial to a newborn baby, my mother made sure I had donor milk on hand when my babies arrived.

The challenge with donor breast milk is acquiring it. This is an awkward conversation to have with female friends, or even friends of friends of friends, who are lactating. Most women don't quite know how to respond when you say, "Hey, I hear you're a good producer. Can I have some of your breast milk?" However, some women are cool with it. Some even sell or donate it, God bless them. I gladly gave my babies what donor milk I was able to find. Not randomly find, I must add. We made sure everyone we received breast milk from was clean and healthy. But I did gladly give the nutritious milk to my babies. And when that ran out, I gave them formula. Society can debate breast-feeding versus formula feeding, but at the end of the day can't we all agree that fed is best?

Two and a half years later, my second born, Charlie James, came two weeks before his due date so I didn't have any donor milk yet. I quickly made a few calls as soon as my contractions began. Within an hour, a friend of a friend stopped by my house with some of her frozen breast milk. In exchange, I gave her a container of formula I had already purchased. We hugged and she wished me the best. Moms supporting moms. Women supporting women.

Exactly two and a half years after Charlie was born, Susie Boesen came along. Susie, named after my mom, was the baby girl I had waited my whole life to meet. However, she was also the won't-sleep-unless-I'm-being-held, always-sick, rash-all-over-my-body, don't-sleep-through-the-night, cry-until-I-get-what-I-want, you-seriously-can't-be-sick-again baby. So, the first year (or three) was rough but we survived.

Teddy, Charlie, and Susie. The little loves of my life. There are days the word love isn't enough to describe my affection for them. On the other hand, there are days I understand why some animals eat their offspring. I'm joking. Kind of. There are days I dream of bottling up their sweetness, their joy, and their innocence because I can't bear the thought of them getting any older. And there are days that I put them to bed at 6:30 p.m., pour myself a bottle of wine, and pretend for 12 hours I don't have children. As Bridget so eloquently says, "Motherhood is such a fragile line between utter bliss and wanting to throw yourself off a cliff."

I am a very open mom. I see the necessity in being open and honest with my children. My philosophy is to talk to your children as often about as much as possible and hope that it makes those awkward adolescent years a little less painful. This philosophy can be attributed to the way I was raised. Although I was not talking about mom's "breasts" at the age of three, her "owies" were often a topic of conversation at the dinner table.

Since the day her breasts came off, we haven't stopped talking about them. And Bridget's. And mine. Even Kathryn's, on occasion.

As openly as I talk to my kids about private parts, I was caught quite off guard one day when Teddy asked me where my nipples were.

The non-mother part of me thought, *How do you know what nipples are and why are you looking at mine!?*

I snapped back to motherhood and realized this was a very real situation. How do I explain to a three-year-old that I had a double prophylactic mastectomy so I wouldn't get breast cancer? In his sweet, innocent three years in this world, to him the extent of an owie was a scrape on the knee. I didn't want to take away that innocence by exposing him to the morbidity of cancer. At the same time, I want my children to grow up knowing about the BRCA1 gene and the impact it has had on our family. I don't want to blindside them when they are 18, or worse, not tell them at all.

So there Teddy and I were, sitting in my bathroom, talking about my nipples. Discussing my lack of nipples with my toddler at the age of three was surprisingly unique, and difficult. I guess I didn't think I would have to have that conversation so young. I was terrified I would say the wrong thing. But what was the right thing to say?

I knelt down and looked Teddy in his bright, innocent eyes. I told him that Mama's breasts could have made Mama very sick and I didn't want to get sick, so I got new breasts. My new breasts looked a little different, but they wouldn't make me sick. Grandma's breasts did make her sick one time, but she is not sick anymore.

Teddy looked back at me with his eyes burrowing into mine. "I don't want you to get sick, Mama."

Me neither, sweet baby, me neither.

PART VI: HOPE IS A GOOD THING

Maybe the best of things.

Dreams Do Come True
Kathryn

Through six years of trying to start a family, we learned to set our expectations low. So low that in preparation for our potential adoption, Bryan and I did not prepare anything. Next to our master bed stood an empty room. We had removed all of the guest bedroom furniture but did not fill it with anything. On a regular basis, I stood in the doorway of this empty room and pictured it filled with a crib, a changing table, and a rocking chair. I wanted a "rustic" theme for this room—it would fit a boy perfectly—and searched the internet for hours, saving items in my wish list. Yet, I refused to buy anything. Lord help me if I ever had to stand there staring at a room full of baby stuff and no baby. I wasn't willing to take that risk, so I did nothing.

In the midst of our fertility struggle, Bridget's daughter, Penelope, was born. Once in a while, I would go over to Bridget's house and ask to put Penelope to bed so I could rock her to sleep. Having Penelope in my arms gave me so much joy and happiness. It taught me about the deep love you can feel for a child and for a sibling. Of anyone in our family, Bridget was the one who understood my pain the most. She listened to me year after year, day after day, and hour after hour. She knew every detail of all of the infertility treatments, every detail of the adoption process, and every detail of my pain.

I think Bridget's heart rivals her strength. Watching her receive her BRCA1 diagnosis and moving forward with unquestionable determination—to prevent cancer, to have the prophylactic mastectomy, even get her tattoos from Whispering Danny—gave me the strength to keep moving forward.

One hot summer evening, we invited the birth parents over for dinner. The birth mom was 32 weeks along and had yet to formally ask us to be the adoptive parents. As we sat around the large island in our kitchen, I heard the words I had been waiting so long to hear.

The fully pregnant teen said softly, "We would like for

you guys to be the adoptive parents of our boy."

I almost cried and wanted to hug them both, but I held myself together. I did, however, blurt out, "We'll name the baby after you guys!"

Bryan nearly fell out of his chair. Sometimes I say things I don't mean out of pure excitement.

I showed them the empty baby's room, including the closet and all the tiny hangers waiting to be filled with onesies. There wasn't much to see but I wanted them to be able to picture where this baby would grow up.

We still had eight long weeks before this baby boy would enter our family. And, I remained skeptical.

I went to doctor's appointments and spent time with the birth mother but deep down inside I was still terrified she would change her mind. I couldn't focus at work; I was so distracted I could hardly carry on a conversation. My head was in the clouds, so much so, that while filling my car with gas one day, I drove off with the pump still attached to my car. Suddenly I heard a sound that can only be described as the sound of metal bending in half. I looked out my rear-view mirror, horrified to see the gas pump hose fly up in the air and gas spewing out everywhere. Luckily, I only did minor damage. This adoption process needed to be wrapped up. I couldn't function like a proper adult.

Finally, two weeks out from the due date, I invited the birth mother to get a pedicure for the big day. While we were both getting a bright shade of pink painted on our toenails, she asked, "Why do you not have anything ready for the baby?"

She had seen the empty baby's room a few weeks prior. I confessed I was honestly scared she might change her mind. Much to my shock, she reassured me she wanted us to have her baby (praise, God!).

We spent the rest of the afternoon deciding on a theme for the baby's room (owls to go with my rustic feel) and shopping for baby supplies. We loaded up the shopping cart with the cutest baby clothes we could find, then ended the afternoon by sitting on the closet floor of the baby's room, filling the empty hangers with signs of life. From that point forward, I was finally able to feel a small amount of joy and happiness throughout a very emotional process.

Soon after, Bryan and I prepared to head to the hospital for our baby to be born. The birth mother was being induced at 9:00am. I carefully picked out my outfit for the day I was to become a mother. I curled my hair and put on my favorite jewelry. Bryan and I hopped in our new SUV, with the car seat snapped in perfectly, a bag for ourselves, and a bag for the baby we had not met yet. I had packed 85 outfits because I couldn't decide which one I wanted him to wear when we left the hospital.

We arrived at the hospital soon after our birth mother checked in. This courageous young girl lay in the hospital bed as we watched her feel every contraction. We talked, we joked around, we sat in silence. We had spent so much time getting to know her that our love for her grew as she was growing our baby. She let us stay in the hospital room until it was time to push. I left my heart in that room the moment I walked out of it.

My family didn't know whether they should come to the hospital or not, since it wasn't me who was having the baby. The whole situation was awkward and unknown. While Bryan and I sat in the waiting room, my phone lit up, a text from Bridget saying that she was downstairs. The moment I saw her, I fell apart. She hugged me while I wept.

I was scared out of my mind that the birth mom would change her mind the minute she saw the face of her newborn son. I was also feeling an intense sense of loss. Many women say they loved being pregnant and the incredible feeling of a baby growing in their body. I had never thought too much about it and was actually slightly relieved that I was not the one pushing a seven-pound baby out of my female parts. However, when I saw our birth mother in labor with our son, I ached to be able to experience what she was going through.

"Why is it not me delivering my firstborn son?" I sobbed to Bridget. "Why did I have to watch someone else do it?" I was a wreck. "This is so much harder than I thought it would be. I am not strong enough to do this."

"Kathryn. You are the bravest person I know. Look at what you have been through and how well you have handled it. Stop thinking about what you can't do and focus on the fact that your son is being born right now. Now is the time for you to get yourself together and go meet your baby boy."

Thank God for sisters.

All the years of work to start a family came down to the surreal wait. I pondered how I would feel to meet our son for the first time. *Will I love him instantly? Will it feel like someone else's baby?* Countless questions that I had tossed around for months ran through my emotionally exhausted brain.

This little boy was about to enter our family without any of our DNA. This concerned me a great deal. *What will he look like? What will he act like? Will he be like Bryan and me, or someone completely different? Will he fit into our family and will our family love him?* I worried for months if he would feel different, like he didn't fit in, when he was older. I also questioned the genetic makeup that he was coming from. The only thing I knew about his birth parents was that they were blonde with blue eyes and their height. *Would he wear glasses? Would he be tall? But most importantly, above all else, would he be happy in our family?* I was overcome with the unknown. The unknown had paralyzed me many times in the past, but I couldn't allow it to paralyze me on one of the most significant days of our life.

While we anxiously waited, one of the nurses on the unit came out to take me back to the nursery. I looked at her confused because we had not heard if our son had been born yet. She told me I needed a wristband to match the baby's band to signify I was the mother.

Me. The mother.

My body didn't ache of sadness anymore. I looked at Bryan cautiously and saw his eyes filling with tears. He could feel it too. He had just become a father.

As the nurse and I walked back to the nursery, she whispered in my ear, "He is perfect."

When we reached the nursery, I saw my mother. She happened to be working that day as a nurse in the same unit where the baby was born. Smiling, she put the wristband on me as I cried uncontrollably.

I returned to the waiting room and showed Bryan the wristband.

"He is perfect," I said.

Bryan said, "Who is perfect?"

"*Our son* is perfect."

The birth mother specifically requested Bryan and I be the first ones to meet the baby. When we saw him—our baby, Briggs Jacob Buckley—all the pain and struggle we went through to start our family disappeared.

We left the hospital with everything we wanted and watched our birth mother get into her car empty-handed. There I was, getting everything I had ever dreamed of, while this teenage girl had just made the hardest, bravest decision of her life. I wept all the way home.

When we walked into our house for the first time as a family of three, I finally felt relieved for the first time in six years. We set our sweet baby boy on the counter in his baby carrier, opened a bottle of wine, and cooked lasagna as our newborn slept peacefully in his new home.

Wow, this motherhood thing is easy, I thought. I've been a mother now for eight years and have never uttered those words since.

I Prayed and He Listened, Damnit
Bridget

I consider myself a believer in God, though I teeter with agnosticism more than I care to admit. I have a relationship with God, and I hope to meet Jesus one day, though convincing me this will happen will take it actually happening. Nonetheless, I talk to God and try my best to be the kindest person I can be (except when people go out of their turn at a four-way stop, of course. Then you'd swear the devil was right here on earth.) While I talk to God almost daily, one particular day I placed a special request. And damnit, He listened.

After Kathryn's final failed attempt at pregnancy, I begged and pleaded with God to please take my fertility and give it to Kathryn.

"Please, God!"

I do not believe we are puppets or that Kathryn's infertility was part of a "plan." We are imperfect beings with imperfect bodies. Due to the imperfections of nature, my body harbors the defective BRCA1 gene. And Kathryn could not conceive despite the most modern of interventions available. I would have given anything to allow Kathryn to experience pregnancy.

I begged God, "Please take any future fertility from me and give it to Kathryn."

At the same time, I really didn't want Penelope to be an only child.

So, I prayed again, "Maybe God, let me have one more first."

Kathryn and Bryan adopted their newborn son, Briggs, on August 28, 2012. Briggs was a gift sent from God (or from the two teenagers who didn't use any birth control). So, Kathryn became a mother.

Then six months after Briggs went home with Kathryn, I gave birth to another child. Penelope is not an only child. Again, thank God. Our son, Abraham, arrived almost exactly two years after our daughter was born.

Abe. Our beautiful baby boy.

But Ryan and I wanted more kids. In true Winn fashion, I didn't want just one child or two children. We Winn sisters wanted *big* families. Is that selfish? Maybe. People would often say to me, "You have a girl and a boy, the perfect family." To me, that was not the perfect family. The perfect family is sprawling with many children and constant chaos.

When Abe was not quite a year old, we tried again for another baby. We got pregnant right away. We lost that pregnancy at five weeks. I started to bleed and knew what was happening. Devastated, I miscarried naturally, and we waited the recommended "one cycle" to try again.

I got pregnant again right away—my fourth pregnancy. My doctor wanted us to come in for an early ultrasound due to the previous loss. I lay in the dark room on the exam table with the transducer on my belly, Ryan standing next to me. An image of our baby popped up on the large TV screen. But its heart rate was low. Too low.

The ultrasound tech nervously stated, "Maybe your dates are off and you're not as far along as you think."

No, I knew. I knew exactly when I got pregnant and that my dates were not off. Something was wrong, again.

I turned to Ryan, weeping. "That's it. There aren't going to be anymore."

The baby didn't survive past seven weeks and I again miscarried. This time, though, I had to endure a dilation and curettage to remove the fetal parts from my uterus because my body wasn't miscarrying on its own. This procedure is done under general anesthesia. I had to wait several days after we found out the baby's heart stopped beating to have the procedure done. I endured several days of carrying around a dead fetus in my uterus. If that isn't hell, I don't know what is.

We met with my doctor a short time later, and she assured me that the two miscarriages were just flukes. She even told me her own story of miscarrying two pregnancies in between her two kids. I was so reassured by her story we got back

NIPPLES OPTIONAL: A MEMOIR

to trying. The next pregnancy turned out to be an ectopic pregnancy—an embryo that has implanted in the fallopian tubes—resulting in another miscarriage.

Hello again, hell.

We met with my doctor again, desperate to know what had happened to my fertility. She told me she was certain I would continue to get pregnant, but she wasn't sure if I would ever carry another baby to term.

"How much more of this can you handle, Bridget?"

I appreciated her going beyond medicine and inserting emotion into the conversation. That doesn't happen very much with doctors and it oddly put me at ease. After three consecutive miscarriages, she suspected something was wrong.

She referred Ryan and me to a local fertility treatment center to undergo further testing. More genetic testing. I thought it quite amusing that I, once reliably fertile, found myself sitting in a fertility clinic. However, even the most invasive (and expensive, may I add) diagnostic studies and labs could not give us an answer. A $3,000 series of genetic testing revealed that I was a chromosomally normal female, and my husband was thrilled to find out he was a chromosomally normal male.

When the nurse called me to give me the results of our genetic testing, she stated the doctor thought we might have the best chances of carrying a healthy baby if we considered in vitro fertilization with preimplantation genetic testing.

"Do you know what IVF is, Bridget?"

My eyes rolled so hard they could have gotten stuck facing the back of my head. I stated that I was, in fact, *very* familiar with IVF.

She then excitedly added, "The great news is that we can test your embryos and throw away the ones that are positive for the BRCA1 mutation!"

Throw away? Throw away my babies because they carry the BRCA gene mutation. Why would I ever do that? I get it. Logically, I get it. But to throw away an embryo because of the mutation would mean that their life wouldn't be worth living. That *my* life wouldn't be worth living because of my mutation. That's just not true. Not even in the slightest.

IVF, PGD, and "throwing away" my babies were not the options for me.

After all of our fertility testing came back normal, we declined IVF. We wanted to try again naturally, just one more time. Like usual, I got pregnant immediately. It was the last pregnancy I would ever experience.

Over the course of about five ultrasounds we literally watched a tiny blob of cells progress nicely into a teeny, tiny baby with a head, arms, legs. We even saw tiny fingers on the ultrasound at nine weeks. My doctor thought we might go ahead and throw in a sixth ultrasound around ten to eleven weeks just to spot check things again.

Ryan was unable to attend the ultrasound due to a work commitment, but that was okay for me because I felt like we were in the clear. My sisters, mother, and Penelope accompanied me, all eager to see the baby. But when the sonographer put the transducer on my belly, there was no movement and no heartbeat. The baby had passed away.

Strangely, I wasn't surprised. I just felt horrified that my mother, sisters and Penelope, *oh God, Penelope*, had to witness such an awful event. Thank goodness Penelope, at the mere age of four, did not realize what was going on. The sonographer quickly whisked her out of the room for a lollipop. She did, however, come to understand that the baby had died. We explained to her that the baby was not going to come home to us but was going to go home to be with Jesus and Grandpa Stillwell.

Ryan and I share a small, silent joke over the fact there are actually four of our babies up in heaven with Grandpa Stillwell, even though he thought this might be his time to finally relax. Instead, he is taking care of his grandbabies. Ryan and I had a good chuckle over that. Humor in tragedy was our way of coping.

I asked myself a billion times, *Why?* Why did this happen?

Why did a perfectly fertile couple with two healthy kids and two picture perfect pregnancies suddenly become incapable of reproducing again?

I pressed the fertility doctor.

"Why is this happening?"

I was desperate for an answer.

She asked me very simply and directly, "Do you know why miscarriages happen?"

I just stared at her, fighting back tears. *Of course, I know why so many miscarriages happen, I have access to Google!* I am asking why *we*, a fertile couple, with two healthy children, have had four miscarriages in a row? Less than one percent of the population suffers from recurrent miscarriages.

She couldn't give me anything. Not even a glimmer of hope. I left the fertility clinic that day and never went back.

Maya Angelou once said, "If you don't like something change it. If you can't change it, change your attitude." I had to change my attitude. So, I prayed. I prayed for peace. I didn't beg this time, I simply said, "Please God, give me peace over this situation."

I said that simple little prayer on Father's Day 2015. Ryan and I took Penelope and Abe to the pool later that evening. As Ryan swam with the kids, I sat on the side of the pool with my feet in the water. I watched them while they laughed and played, admiring them.

Is this our family? Maybe this is.

This is perfect.

A weight lifted off of my shoulders at that moment. We *did* have the perfect family. Did God help me see their perfection at the pool that evening, or did I come to it on my own? Did God actually listen when I begged him to take my fertility and give it to Kathryn? Again, I don't believe we are puppets for God, but I can't help but wonder.

Warrior not Worrier
Maureen

I go back and forth about whether or not a prophylactic double mastectomy is actually a battle or a blessing from God. One thing I know for sure is that it changed me. The physical changes are obvious and to be expected. Those changes also look pretty good in a low-cut dress. It is the psychological changes that really surprised me.

Example 1: Hypochondria

I could be wrong, but I don't believe I was a hypochondriac before I found out about the BRCA1 gene. I know I am one now. And I am okay with that. Mostly because the diseases and cancers I "develop," end up "curing" themselves. My body has "cured" itself of brain, stomach, leg, ovarian, colon and bone cancer. It is truly a miracle.

The one thing my body has not cured itself of is hypochondria. The irony is that before finding out about the gene, I didn't have a care in the world. I have always been somewhat of a type A personality and have always tried my best to be successful, but never before did I worry about my health like I do now. My foot hurts? Foot cancer. My elbow hurts? Elbow cancer. What I have found (or what Josh has pointed out to me) is that, to me, it is either nothing or cancer. There is nothing in between. I'll admit, I am a little cancer phobic. Which is the exact reason I attribute my hypochondria back to the gene. But like I said, I am okay with that. If the gene has led to my hypochondria, which leads me to the doctor who is able to explain that my elbow hurts because I played tennis yesterday, that is good news. If hypochondria helps me be preventative and vocal about my health, then it has served me well.

Example 2: Anticipatory Anxiety

Anticipatory Anxiety, or AA as I like to call it, is also a self-diagnosed term that refers to the fear of looming death; i.e. a tornado that demolishes your house, or a freak earthquake in Kansas. This syndrome is similar to anxiety, although no real event is occurring; it is merely the fear that something could potentially take place sometime in the future. AA goes hand in hand with hypochondria. I believe my AA has gotten worse, not only because of the gene but also because I have more to lose, more loved ones to care about, more to live for.

Fortunately, I am not alone in the battle of AA; Bridget, too, struggles with it. Most of our conversations revolve around this topic.

"Where should our family meeting place be, in case of emergency?"

"What type of emergency are we talking about?"

"The world gets destroyed."

"Canada, definitely Canada."

Usually the world does not get destroyed and we laugh about our insanity while knowing that when the world does get destroyed, we will know where to meet.

I have always described myself as a worrier, although I never believed I had a true anxiety disorder. This changed after Josh and I moved from Omaha (where we had lived for ten years) to Kansas City (the city where we both grew up). I knew I would miss Omaha and the life we had created there, although great things awaited us in Kansas. Our children would grow up with their cousins, a luxury I never had, and they would have a memorable relationship with their grandparents. Again, a privilege I missed out on. I would live in the same city as my sisters, something I had dreamed of for years.

Coincidentally, the year we moved back to Kansas I gave birth to my second son, Charlie. It was also the year I quit a job I loved after seven years. Within a matter of six months, Josh and I owned a new house, worked at new jobs, lived in a new city with a toddler and a new baby.

All of this meant stress, and for the first time in my life, it meant debilitating anxiety.

I had traveled the country, I had traveled the world, I had boarded a plane to New Zealand without knowing a single person on it... and then one day I couldn't go on a run. I couldn't do the simplest of tasks without anxiety flooding my mind. I became paralyzed with fear. I feared not being able to get out of the grocery store, as if I didn't have control over it. While this is a completely irrational thought to someone without anxiety, it was the world I was living in. Call me crazy. Some people did.

Fortunately, and sadly, I wasn't alone in the intense anxiety battle. My brother, Paul, has battled severe anxiety since college. Even though we haven't lived in the same city in nearly two decades, at times I feel closer to him than anyone else in the world. I can call Paul when I am at my weakest, and he immediately makes me feel like I am not alone. I can be 100% myself when I talk to him and never feel judged. Paul provides me love and support by simply answering the phone.

With the exception of our gender and his mad musical skills, Paul and I are nearly identical. In addition to our raging eczema, love for old houses, and individualistic personalities, we both have restlessly creative minds.

When my anxiety struck, Paul was the first person I called. I so badly needed advice, guidance, and reassurance.

"I'm not anxious. But I am just worried I will be anxious," I cried.

"That's anxiety," he explained.

"Well, fuck."

Although he was able to provide me understanding and comfort, he wasn't able to take the anxiety away. He did, however, send me a book entitled, *The Anxiety and Phobia Workbook*. Reading the book made me feel even worse, like I was suffering from a severe mental illness. Maybe I was, but at the time I wanted to believe my anxiety was situational, simply resulting from the stress I was under and the dramatic change we had just endured.

What I did learn from the book was that new research indicates anxiety may be genetic.

Damn genetics again.

In fact, experts are beginning to believe that anxiety may be correlated to the length of the 17th chromosome, the same chromosome that carried BRCA1. *Damn that 17th chromosome again.* I am no scientist, but this is more than a coincidence. At the same time, it didn't really matter to me. I didn't care whether my anxiety was genetic or environmental. I just needed to know how to deal with it.

Unfortunately, what the book didn't do was cure my anxiety. It didn't tell me whether or not to quit my job, which was giving me additional stress. One day at work my boss shared her thoughts on my condition. She sat me down and said bluntly, "I'm disappointed you have this little anxiety monster."

You and me both, sister. You and me both.

The book didn't tell me if I needed daily medication. It didn't tell me if I would ever feel "normal" again. These were all questions I had to answer for myself.

During this time, I occasionally drove to my parents' house. When I walked in the door and saw my father reading the newspaper in the kitchen, comfort instantly swept over me. My father is a great combination of being both logical and emotional, characteristics I like to think I inherited from him. He helped me cope with anxiety by encouraging me to not dwell on the "why." I had to focus on the "what now..." For me and my father, the "what now" meant sharing coffee on Friday mornings.

This created a new routine for me. Week by week, my father provided me guidance and helped me find my way out of my darkest of dark days.

My anxiety didn't kill me. Some days, I thought it would. Some days, it felt like it might. But it never did. And, with time, it got better. Not all at once and not completely. But every day was a little easier than the last (except for days I have to fly on a plane, those are never good days).

What I learned was that although many things had changed in my life, many things hadn't. I still had those same sweet, curly haired boys to make me laugh uncontrollably and my sweet and sour Susie Boesen. I still had Josh, my constant, to remind me to slow down, be patient and take a Xanax if I needed to. And, deep down, I was still me. I still had the same wit, sense of humor, and optimism that had helped me endure tribulations before.

Most importantly, I learned not to fear change. Change can be scary and hard. So damn hard. But life is constantly changing. Author Ritu Ghatourey says, "You fall, you rise, you make mistakes, you live, you learn. You're human, not perfect. You've been hurt, but you're alive. Think of what a precious privilege it is to be alive, to breathe, to think, to enjoy, and to be with people you love. Sometimes there is sadness in our journey, but there is also lots of beauty. We must keep putting one foot in front of the other even when we hurt, for we will never know what is waiting for us just around the bend." I had to push through the anxiety and fear and worry to see the beauty in life. I had to be a warrior to overcome my worry.

I learned that just because the philosophy "What doesn't kill you, makes you stronger" is true, it doesn't make the fight any easier. Maybe I went through this dark time so I could gain strength for my future. Because what waited for me around the next bend rivaled anything I'd been through so far.

PART VII: TWISTS AND TURNS IN THE ROAD

Healing isn't always linear.

Back Down the Road
Kathryn

I don't believe everything happens for a reason. Life doesn't always make sense when you are going through it. But I do believe we can find good in all the things that happen, even if we have to look really hard.

My sisters both had baby boys within six months of us bringing Briggs home from the hospital. Raising these handsome boys together, with my two best friends, was worth all of our waiting. Our brother, Paul, and his wife also had a daughter during this same time. And although they live far away, experiencing parenthood together as siblings has been a sweet blessing. John C. Maxwell said it best when he said, "Think back to the most important experience of your life, the highest highs, the greatest victories, the most daunting obstacles overcome. How many happened to you alone? I bet there are very few. When you understand that being connected to others is one of life's greatest joys, you realize that life's best comes when you initiate and invest in solid relationships."

My family was beyond supportive of our entire fertility journey and the adoption process, even in the midst of their own pain. So when we told them we were going to attempt IVF for a fifth time, in an attempt to give Briggs a sibling, they didn't question it.

Back down the fertility road we went.

Briggs was one year old when we traveled to a fertility clinic in Denver. The Colorado Center for Reproductive Medicine (CCRM) is the top-rated fertility clinic in the United States. Because my infertility was still unexplainable, we went to Denver with the idea that we would use an egg from another woman and Bryan's sperm. I already knew that I wanted a cute little blonde girl (so Briggs could have a blonde sibling and little because I didn't want to carry a large baby).

After one day of testing, the Denver fertility clinic was able to determine why we were not getting pregnant. And much to my astonishment, they could try to fix the issue. According to the Colorado Center for Reproductive Medicine, I was missing a "beta 3 integrin," which is basically the glue in a woman's uterine lining that attaches the embryo to the uterus.[xix]

Since my mom never had trouble getting pregnant, I don't believe this was something I inherited—or didn't inherit—but it certainly begs the question: "Why is the gene that creates this glue turned off during the implantation phase of my cycle?"

I asked the doctor if this was something that could be genetic.

In short, his answer was, "We (CCRM) don't know that yet. Identifying this missing protein in a woman is very new, so new that most infertility clinics are not willing to even test for it." This explained why my infertility clinic in Kansas City was not willing to do additional testing on me. There just wasn't enough information, and this was a rare issue. But, in my own defense, I had been onto something when I asked my clinic in Kansas City a few years prior if there was any additional testing that we could do. I would never take back the adoption process, but I do wish I had been brave enough to seek a second opinion sooner in the midst of our infertility struggles.

The supposedly straightforward fix to get the beta 3 integrin back into my uterus took a few months. First, prescription drugs sent my body into menopause for 60 days. Then I went off of the drug so my body could reset itself. I nearly lost my mind while going through forced menopause.

One morning Bryan woke up in a pool of my sweat.

"What is happening to your body?" He probably wondered about my mind, too, but was smart enough not to prod.

"I am in hell. Pure hell."

Horribly agitated, I gained weight faster than I could take it off and felt downright miserable. Bryan took this as an opportunity to buy me some new pajamas that had less material, thinking that would solve my sweating problem. I was not amused.

Once the beta 3 integrin returned to my uterus, I started

the IVF process again.

The doctor retrieved twelve eggs and fertilized eight of them with Bryan's sperm. We ended up with six perfectly normal embryos to be frozen while my body healed and prepared for the transfer.

I was baffled. The doctor in Kansas City had told us our genetic testing revealed almost all of our embryos were chromosomally abnormal. Could the genetic testing that we had done in prior IVF cycles been wrong? The PDG (genetic) testing on embryos was a relatively new technology. I guess we'll never know.

Several months later, Bryan and I headed back to Denver to transfer in our two perfect little unthawed embryos. After seeing our little guys under the microscope, I lay back down on the cold hospital table, shut my eyes, and said a little prayer.

Then came the wait to find out if it worked. Just two short weeks and no wine.

Ten days into the two-week wait, I did exactly what the doctors told me not to do. I took a pregnancy test. I flew out of the bathroom and shoved the test in Bryan's face.

"It worked. I am pregnant!"

"What? How can you tell me this now? I am running late to a meeting at work."

Note to self: Stop springing things on Bryan. A heads up that I was taking a pregnancy test would have been a good idea.

The doctors knew the sex of the two embryos they transferred in but would not tell us until we had a positive pregnancy test via blood work. I went to the clinic on the 14th day to have my blood drawn, and then returned home to wait for the official results.

The blood work would not tell us if both embryos survived, but if the hCG (Human Chorionic Gonadotropin) number was in a certain range, it would signify the possibility of twins.

Finally, as I put Briggs down for his afternoon nap, my phone rang. I quickly shut his door and sat on the stairs leading downstairs. Our house was only three years old and still smelled brand new with fluffy and clean carpet, yet to be destroyed by dirty toddlers. I leaned against the wrought iron railing as the doctor spoke.

"Congratulations, you are pregnant!"

The doctor went on to tell me that my hCG level was higher than the normal range, which would suggest it could be twins but we would not know anything until the sonogram at twelve weeks. The doctor also told me that he transferred a male and a female embryo. *A boy and a girl.*

Turns out, only one baby showed up on the twelve-week sonogram. The sonogram technician showed me where the second baby tried to implant but did not make it.

The idea of a baby not making it pained me. At the time of all of this, Bridget was experiencing this exact feeling with another miscarriage. I had suffered so much pain through my infertility journey, but never had I lost a baby. The devastation that goes along with miscarriage is an inexplicable loss that feels so unjustified.

At our next routine sonogram a few weeks later, the technician stopped mid-sonogram to bring in the doctor. Magically, an older gentleman with white hair and a lab coat appeared. I had had enough sonograms to know that the doctor appearing mid-sonogram was not normal. I carefully studied the doctor's face as he delicately measured something on our baby over and over. After what felt like a lifetime, the doctor invited me to get dressed and have a seat on the couch on the other side of the room so we could talk. I looked at Bryan with deep concern as he helped me off of the table.

The doctor explained that our baby had an oversized ventricle in the back of its brain. The ventricle that was "too large" could be a sign of fluid on the brain which could result in some developmental and learning delays. The important thing for us to know was that this was something that may resolve itself during the pregnancy, or it could turn into something that would impact this baby for the rest of its life.

I began to doubt myself, my marriage and my life. Was

Bryan right? Did we force the hand in having a family? Maybe we should have left it alone. Could our marriage survive a special needs child? We barely survived five IVF procedures and an adoption.

I also felt so much animosity towards all of my friends who had had easy, healthy pregnancies. At this point, I was over halfway through my pregnancy, I was fat, I had 85 cavities from all of the candy I was consuming, and I hated life.

If the Uterus is Optional...Opt Out
Bridget

I used to really like my uterus. She was so kind to me with my periods. They were light and brief. I never understood the mind-numbingly painful cramps that some of my friends described. I might have gotten a slight discomfort a day before my period came, as a gentle and friendly reminder to throw a tampon in my purse.

Thanks, body! I would think to myself. *Gosh, you're great!*

I even knew exactly when I ovulated. So much so, that I never needed to use those pricey ovulation kits or temperature method or check my cervix or whatever people do to know when that little egg drops. I managed to get pregnant six times with very little effort. And trust me, I am not bragging for two reasons: 1) Witnessing Kathryn's infertility showed me how agonizing it can be to have a negative pregnancy test month after month, and 2) Out of six pregnancies, I only hold two of those babies in my arms.

My uterus made a great home for the two most incredible people on the planet. Penelope and Abe developed in a warm, cozy place and most importantly, they were safe.

Then for reasons I will never know, my uterus decided she didn't want to grow any more babies. Three of the four pregnancies that we lost implanted nicely, even developed heartbeats. Statistics show that once a fetus develops a heartbeat, the chance of that pregnancy being successful is nearly 80%. *What the hell, uterus?* My babies had heartbeats. Knowing that breaks my heart.

When I finally came to terms with the fact my uterus was no longer going to make a nice home for any more babies, I considered giving her the boot.

Being BRCA1 mutation positive, it is recommended the ovaries be removed by the age of 35. Most of the time, when the ovaries go, the uterus and fallopian tubes go with them (even though there is limited evidence to support that ovarian cancer may originate in the fallopian tubes—more research needs to be done on this). But when I had my ovaries and fallopian removed, I was a very, very stupid woman and opted to keep my uterus.

The reasoning behind this was quite silly, although necessary. The gynecologic-oncologist (GYNONC) insisted I take eight weeks off of work to recover from a complete hysterectomy. I was set to start a new job and didn't want to set that date back two entire months, so she advised we only remove the ovaries and fallopian tubes. A *bilateral salpingo-oophorectomy*, she called it, and assured me it was a simple surgery and recovery. I could do the uterus at a later date when I had time.

When ovaries are removed from a woman's body, the hormones go with it. Hormone replacement isn't just important for the physical symptoms that accompany menopause, but important for a young woman's bone, heart, and neurological health. However, my doctor made it very clear that she would not start hormone replacement therapy until six weeks after my surgery. She was very conservative and didn't want to increase any risk for blood clots post-surgery. Sure, I could get on board with that. I liked a careful doctor. I don't like blood clots.

So, yes, that is what we would do. Surgery, menopause, hormone therapy. Easy enough. The very nice, but very young, GYNONC also explained that hormone therapy would consist of a low dose estrogen/progesterone patch. Again, easy enough.

The day of surgery to remove my ovaries and fallopian tubes, my husband and I arrived at the hospital early while it was still dark outside, just as we had done the days Penelope and Abe were born. We checked in and they led me to pre-op.

It is common practice for a pregnancy test to be administered prior to any fertile female's surgery. I secretly prayed for it to be positive. If it was, I could skip out of the hospital. "No surgery for me to end my fertility because I'm pregnant!"

The nurse came by while I was changing into my gown for surgery. "Good news, your pregnancy test is negative." It was a farfetched dream for an unplanned pregnancy to get me out of the oophorectomy, I know. But I could still hope.

I chose to eliminate my extra high risk of developing ovarian cancer, but it wasn't my choice to stop having children. *I want it to be my choice!* I silently wept in the pre-operating area.

The nurse glanced up from her clipboard. "Are you scared, honey?"

No, I am not scared. I am sad. I am so damn sad.

Just as I had said to my mother years earlier before my mastectomy, I made sure my husband understood that if anything unexpected happened in surgery and I was left a vegetable, he must make the decision to pull the plug.

"I repeat, pull the plug."

He said, "I'll see you in a little bit and love you."

"Pull the plug," I gently reminded him again as I was being wheeled away. He just smirked.

I woke up in the post-operative area sometime later very itchy, very irritable, and blind. My nurse was male. I am not against male nurses by any means. My brother is a male nurse. But this guy was not gentle, empathetic, or sympathetic. He kept telling me to calm down, but I didn't have my glasses and I couldn't see anything. I was also alone. They had not let Ryan back yet. As a nurse and now nurse practitioner, I have always been taught to listen to the patient—they will tell you what is wrong with them.

When the anesthesiologist came by to check on me—also a male, by the way— he noticed I was agitated and asked what he could do to help. I said I am in pain and I can't see anything because I don't have my glasses. He was very friendly and asked the nurse to get me my glasses and some pain medication. After that, I was much better.

About two weeks after my oophorectomy I was getting ready to go to bed when I felt a large gush from down under. I went to the bathroom and a large amount of bright red blood surged out of me. I put a pad in my underwear and tried to go back to bed, but again felt a large gush of blood. I expressed concern to Ryan.

"Just try to go to sleep... it'll be fine."

"Um, no! I am going to wake up in a pool of blood, half dead!"

I used my better judgment and called the on-call physician associated with my GYNONC. I should mention that the hospital where I had my surgery was a teaching hospital. This means residents staffed the night shift. Now I am sure most residents are great, professional, and smart. However, the one I got on the phone was none of those things. Her recommendation was the same as my husband's, who has no medical training. I urged that I literally could not get off of the toilet because the blood would not stop flowing.

Exasperated, she grunted, "Okay, if you want to come in, you can."

I asked if I should drive thirty minutes to the hospital where I had surgery, or should I go to a closer hospital (one where my friend's husband was an ER doc and he could help me.) The resident suggested I go somewhere close to home (*Wrong! PSA: If possible, go to the hospital where you had surgery.*)

My friend's husband was unfortunately not working when I went into the local hospital, but he called in before I arrived and talked to the other female doctor on the night shift. He assured me she would take care of me. After six hours in the ER and one CT scan that showed active bleeding, she stated, "Something has ripped open inside and you are probably going back to surgery tonight. We need to send you by ambulance right now to the hospital where you had surgery."

A little while later the EMTs came in to transport me. When we arrived at the next hospital, the security guard wanded my body with a metal detector as I was being brought into the hospital on a stretcher. *I'm clinging to life! How could I have time to be concealing a weapon or the energy to do anything with it if I had one?* I get it, he was doing his job. Also, I wasn't clinging to life. I'm just being dramatic.

The resident who had answered the phone (I'll call her Dr. Ding-a-ling) came to see me after I was admitted and did a pelvic exam. Blood continued to cascade.

"Wow, you are bleeding!"

Uh, yeah. I am. That's what I tried to tell you seven hours ago when you told me to go to bed.

She got out her cell phone and took a picture of the blood, texted the picture to my surgeon and assured me she would promptly delete it. My hemoglobin had dropped from 15 to 12 in a matter of hours. If it dropped any lower, they were going to give me a blood transfusion.

A few hours later, I lay in a hospital bed, surrounded by my doctor and 27 med students. Fine, 10 med students. I hadn't slept in 48 hours. I had gone to bed with my hair wet the night before, so you can imagine what I looked like. One very out of character thing I had done the night before was shave my legs. *Bravo, me.* The phlebotomist came to draw my blood. She said to me, "I never get down about my life when I look at patients like you." This confirmed my suspicion that I looked like shit. Awesome.

My doctor (and all her little med students) determined that nothing had actually ripped open during my recovery. This was, in fact, not even possible my doctor informed me. Apparently, my body experienced a rare complication from surgery. My uterus was missing her two friends—the ovaries—and went AWOL. She abandoned her duties to my body and retaliated by hemorrhaging. The bleeding finally subsided when the doctor put me on birth control to replace some of the missing hormones. I was discharged from the hospital later that evening.

My Idle Tuesday
Maureen

"Don't worry about the future;
or worry,
but know that worrying is as effective as trying to solve an
algebra equation by chewing bubblegum.
The real troubles in your life are apt to be things that never
crossed your worried mind, the kind that blindside you at
4:00 p.m. on some idle Tuesday."

Mary Schmich was right when she wrote this in her
1997 Chicago Tribune article (most commonly remembered as
titled: "Wear Sunscreen.[xx]") The real troubles in your life *are*
the things that never cross your mind. They aren't the countless
doubts and uncertainties that keep us up at night. Did I lock the
back door? Do my children love me? Do my parents know I love
them? Am I raising a psychopath? (No, just me?)

The real troubles are the curveballs, the ones that blindside you on an idle Tuesday. We all have them, we all know they
are coming. But when, and what will they be?

My idle Tuesday came on September 19, 2018.

Four weeks prior, I met with a genetic counselor to get
tested for the BRCA1 gene mutation. This seems quite silly for
someone who has known since they were 21 that they were
BRCA1 positive and who has already undergone a prophylactic
mastectomy. The test was a minor formality, actually, to comply with insurance in preparation for my next surgery.

While I had reduced my risk of breast cancer from 80+
% to 1% by having a mastectomy, my ovaries still had a battle to fight. And they were becoming a ticking time bomb with
each passing year. I had grown up knowing that I needed to get
married young, have my children young and get my ovaries out
young. So, I did as I was told. I married sweet Josh, had three
beautiful babies and prepared myself for a total hysterectomy
plus bilateral salpingo oophorectomy (BSO). This surgery is the

complete removal of the ovaries, fallopian tubes and uterus.

I was only 32 years old and I knew I still had three more good years with my natural hormones. In fact, my doctor recommended I wait until I was 35 to have the surgery. But I was done having my babies. My youngest, and only daughter, Susie, sealed the deal on the thought of another baby. Seriously. I won't go into the details, but it was enough for Josh to schedule a vasectomy on his own. In retrospect, I don't think we even had a discussion to make sure it was the right decision for us. He just scheduled it and asked me to pick him up from the doctor. Funny enough, I couldn't, and he had to get a ride home.

Our family was complete. Time to move on to the next chapter of our lives.

The beginning of our next chapter was going to begin with another life changing surgery. While a hysterectomy is less complex than a mastectomy, the effects of it can be more severe. Essentially, the majority of your hormones are removed from your body, which sends you into immediate menopause. Hormones don't just have an effect on your sex drive or ability to reproduce. They have an impact on every single type of tissue in your body, ranging from skin health to cognition and memory.[xxi] While hormone replacement can help curb the effects of menopause, the transition can be slow and difficult. This major surgery also signifies the end of your childbearing years and the removal of the key organs that symbolize your femininity.

Knowing this, I started the process slowly. My first stop was with a genetic counselor at the University of Kansas. My insurance needed to see genetic test results that showed I was positive. The results from Dr. Lynch's research study would not suffice because they were from a research lab, not a commercial lab. So, I called my genetic counselor and set up a test that I already knew I would fail.

When I went to have my test done, the genetic counselor treated me like a typical patient. We reviewed my family history and she explained BRCA to me like it was new information.

This time, however, I was educated enough to ask questions and understand the implications. She said she would call me in two weeks with the results but to expect them to be the same as my original test.

Four weeks passed and I began to worry. So, I emailed my genetic counselor. She replied and said she would call me in the morning. Immediately, my mind began to race. My anxiety spiked. *Maybe my results were worse than a BRCA mutation. What can be worse than being BRCA positive?* (A lot of things, actually.)

What I did not expect was the news the geneticist gave me when she called the next morning. It was 10:02 in the morning and, to everyone else, it was a typical Tuesday morning. But, for me, this was my idle Tuesday. News was on its way.

"Hello?" I spoke hesitantly.

"Maureen, we need to talk."

I rushed into a vacant conference room near my desk, wanting to conceal my reaction from my coworkers.

"You're negative," The genetic counselor stated.

I dropped the phone. I never saw that curveball coming.

The conference room was not soundproof and was lined with glass windows. From across the office, my boss saw me crying. He came in to make sure I was okay.

Until then, no one knew a lot about my genetic results and my subsequent surgery. *Where do I begin, I wonder?*

I blurted out, "I'm not BRCA positive!"

Of course, he looked confused. To most, that was good news.

"And that's a bad thing?" he asked, attempting to be supportive but clearly baffled.

I couldn't articulate my thoughts and feelings. I had to get out of that room. Immediately, I grabbed my computer and told my boss I would be back tomorrow.

Intrinsically, I drove to Bridget's house. I apologized over and over again for being BRCA1 negative while I sat in her kitchen and cried. She silently hugged me for what seemed like hours. Then she looked me in the eye and said, "Don't be sorry.

This is good news. This is the news we always dreamed of hearing."

While she was right, I still couldn't help feeling guilty that I had somehow escaped the dreaded fate that she still lived in.

It suddenly dawned on me that if this impacted me so greatly, it would likely impact my parents just the same. They happened to be traveling in China at the time and it was the middle of the night there. But they needed to know, and I needed their support.

My mother, half asleep, could only utter the words, "What the hell?"

My thoughts exactly.

For me, the news was incredibly difficult to process. I should have been doing cartwheels down the street. *Why was I not doing cartwheels down the street?*

I was in a daze of disbelief. That's why. I was told there was no chance my initial results were wrong. In 2008, I looked Dr. Lynch in the eye and asked him if there was any possibility that his results were wrong. He told me no. And *he was wrong.*

Finding out I was BRCA1 negative was more shocking than finding out I was positive. My inaccurate original test result added an unnecessary burden to my life that I had carried around for more than a decade. I made major decisions based on a false positive. As I processed this news, I could feel every emotion yet nothing all at once.

I suppose I should have felt grateful. But was I? I was grateful when l knew I was BRCA1 positive because, like my mom always says, knowledge is power. But I wasn't BRCA1 positive anymore. I was grateful that my mastectomy went well. I was grateful for a supportive husband. I was grateful for my two boys who are healthy enough to run around the house like maniacs, and my sweet baby girl. I was grateful my baby girl wouldn't inherit this gene now that I didn't carry it. I always knew that the risk of passing the BRCA1 gene mutation on to a child existed, but the reality was much more difficult after I met these sweet miracles. It felt more like guilt than simple genetics. But, alas, my sweet Susie and two feisty boys would not have to carry this burden and, yes, for that, I was grateful.

However, I wasn't grateful that I didn't get to breastfeed my babies. I have felt my babies kick inside of me. I have felt the indescribable pain of a contraction. But I will never feel myself nourishing my babies. My inaccurate test results took that away from me. Even worse, it took my breasts from me. I thought I had no choice but to have my breasts removed. Did I lose them in vain?

I felt so conflicted. I had lived my life as a previvor; I wore it like a fucking badge of honor. And then what!? Who was I? *What* was I? My whole life I had felt so proud to tell this story, to be part of this study, to make a difference. Not only was that study incorrect, but I could no longer call myself a previvor. That title was stolen from me in an instant. Moreover, as a daughter and a sister, my previvor title and BRCA status connected me to my family. It was our cross to bear together. We were a club, albeit a club I would not choose to be part of, but a club, nonetheless. I have stood in locked arms with my siblings and parents since I first found out I was positive. We fought this fight together. Now I had abandoned Bridget. No longer did she have a sister who shared the mutated gene. Bridget was now the only Winn sister who was BRCA1 positive. I had a hard time wrapping my mind around that. And I no longer shared the same notorious claim to fame as my mother. We had always been identical in every way, including, maybe even especially, our inner fight with BRCA1. What was my purpose now?

It's Okay to be Sad
Kathryn

One fall evening as I neared my final trimester, I took a drink of water, but I couldn't feel it. There wasn't any water in my mouth to swallow. When I looked down, I saw the water had spilled down the front of my shirt and over my growing belly.

Confused, I took another drink. Again, the water poured out of my mouth and down my shirt. Immediately, I rushed to the bathroom and looked in the mirror.

The entire left side of my face was drooping. Petrified, I called the doctor. She said not to panic—it was likely not a stroke—and ordered me directly to the ER.

"Bryan!" I screamed. "I need to go to the ER!"

Without a word, he grabbed Briggs out of his highchair, loaded him in the car and drove me directly to the hospital. He saw my face and heard my voice and knew this was serious. I had lost all senses on the left side of my face. I couldn't taste anything on the left side of my tongue, I couldn't hear out of my left ear, I couldn't smell out my left nostril. My left eye wouldn't close, and my cheek and lips drooped.

In the hospital, we learned I was not having a stroke, but was suffering from Bell's Palsy: a temporary weakness or paralysis on one side of the face.[xxii] This typically happens when a nerve becomes inflamed or compressed. The symptoms could resolve in a matter of weeks to months or could be permanent. I was six months pregnant, miserable, fat, dispirited—and now paralyzed in my face. Once again, I felt like a teenager wanting to hide my hideous face, except this time because of Bell's Palsy instead of flat warts.

The baby was due on New Year's Eve, exactly four years after we started the adoption process for Briggs. My doctor reluctantly agreed to deliver our baby the day after Christmas to put me out of my misery. On Christmas night, I went into the hospital to be induced. It took a while for labor to progress, even with the contract-inducing drug Pitocin. Apparently, this baby was not in a hurry to join this world. (Talk about fore-shadowing. Daily he lays in his bed, wrapped tightly in his covers, and tells me how much he does not want to get out of bed to go to school.)

Late that evening, things became serious when my blood pressure began to drop. I cried in pain, as if the epidural had been put in wrong. I went back and forth between passing out and vomiting. My doctor suggested we do a C-section immediately. During the C-section, all I remember is crying and saying something isn't right, then I completely passed out.

When I finally came to, I found myself tucked into a hospital bed holding our baby boy, Beau. I had given birth, an accomplishment I had longed for, fought for. An accomplishment I never knew would be so difficult to attain. My life was now complete.

The next day the doctor ordered an ultrasound of Beau's brain to determine why his ventricles were enlarged. The ultrasound displayed two large brain bleeds on one side of his brain. Only a brain MRI could tell us how serious this was. The hospital where I delivered was not capable of performing a brain MRI on an infant, so Beau was transferred via ambulance to the local Children's Hospital for an MRI scan of his brain. Bryan went with Beau and I stayed in the hospital. Bridget sat on the hospital bed with me waiting. For hours. She consoled me. She encouraged me. She kept me from losing my mind. As we waited, I could hardly breathe. I was more scared than I have ever been in my life.

Finally, Bryan called. "Your baby boy is coming home!!"

Miraculously, the scan at the Children's Hospital showed no evidence of a brain bleed and the ventricle was the correct size. Beau was 100% fine.

Bryan cried. I cried. Bridget cried. Even the nurse in the room at the time cried. It was a true miracle.

Bringing Beau home was slightly different than Briggs. I didn't have the energy to even look at a bottle of wine, let alone cook lasagna. Was it easy? Hell no. Was it worth it? Yes. Every bit of it.

Beau was four months old when we received a letter from the fertility clinic in Denver. What did we want to do with our four frozen remaining embryos? Save them and pay the annual room and board fee (about $700), destroy them, or donate them to science?

Even through the challenges of infertility treatments, I always thought we would have a big family. I wanted more than two kids. To me, those embryos were little Beaus. The idea of destroying them nearly took my breath away every time I thought about it.

At the time, I was trying to breastfeed Beau while simultaneously pumping milk for Maureen's soon-to-be new baby. Maureen was pregnant with baby number two and since she couldn't breastfeed because of her double mastectomy, I offered to help feed her baby. Our mother had been purchasing milk off of the black market to feed Bridget and Maureen's babies, so I used this as my opportunity to chip in. (Actually, buying breast milk is not illegal but many hospitals did not, at that time, approve of breast milk from a different mother because it wasn't able to be screened or follow any protocols. So, selling and buying it was not a problem. The problem was bringing it into the hospital.)

I have always felt guilty for not having to deal with the BRCA1 gene like my sisters have. No cancer scares. No prophylactic mastectomy. My breasts and nipples remain intact (albeit smaller than what I'd choose if I could). Sometimes I feel like an outsider in my family. I don't personally know what it feels like to carry around the burden of this gene mutation. For most of my life, I was the only sibling who didn't carry it. Up until Maureen's reversed BRCA1 diagnosis (which shocked the entire family), BRCA1 bonded my mother and all of my siblings. My dad and I are the only ones who have not been told we carry a defective gene. Consequently, I have never had to make the decision to alter my life, or my body, because of it. Granted, experiencing infertility was not without its difficulties, but it was not life threatening.

I suspect my mom knew I had felt this way. She constantly reminded us that if everyone threw their problems in a bowl and you got to choose which one you wanted, you would most likely choose your own. I agree with this statement. But it still didn't erase my deep desire to relate to my sisters, or more importantly, to take this horrible gene mutation away from them.

To be an active part of my family's BRCA1 journey, I took on the assignment of pumping milk for Maureen's baby as my mission. A mission that failed. Breastfeeding was a complete disaster for me, but I was so hell bent on making it work that I made my life and everyone's around me miserable. Beau woke often through the night, Briggs didn't yet understand why he had a baby brother in the house, and I felt exhausted, grumpy, and annoyed. Bryan worked hard, only to come home to a wife who handed him two children.

I likely only supplied Maureen's little boy with a few days of milk and eventually gave up. By this time, it was either save my marriage or save milk for Maureen. I chose my marriage.

We chose to keep the embryos for the next year, per my insistence, not Bryan's. I needed more time to make this important decision. After marriage counseling and some rest, I learned an important truth about myself. Our past, living a life surrounded by infertility treatments, was over. It had become so much of who I was that I was afraid to let it go and move on. Yes, I felt sad about not holding another new baby in my arms, especially now that my little boys were growing up so quickly. But as a friend reminded me, it's okay to be sad when the season of babies is over. And I agonized over discarding the embryos, but I was done.

"Bryan, I am ready to donate our embryos to science."

His reply shocked me. "I was going to tell you I am ready to reschedule our IVF appointment."

I was 38 and by the time we went through all of it, I would be 40 with a newborn. He understood this and as we talked through it, we decided we both had to grieve the loss of these embryos and that this era was over for us. In the end, we both arrived at the same decision and signed the forms to have our embryos donated to science.

Our boys are eight and six as of this writing. They are happy and healthy. In spite of all the obstacles, setbacks, quarrels, and painful decisions, our adoption adventure and infertility journey led us here. I could have never predicted our family would come together this way, but I'm so very, very happy it did.

Whatever Lies Ahead
Bridget

The birth control pill made me feel terrible, so my GYNONC suggested we try the hormone patch. But it kept falling off and sticking to my clothes. I never made it through a workout without it falling off. My GYNONC's nurse suggested sticking it in different places on my body.

"I have put this everywhere but on my forehead," I complained. "It will not stay on me."

The doctor then sent me a message that read: "We suggest you establish care with a gynecologist who will be able to further manage your care."

"Hey Doc, I am a BRCA mutation carrier who has had a preventative bilateral mastectomy, and now oophorectomy. I have been pregnant six times and have had three D&Cs. I have undergone eight different surgeries in my 30-something years on this earth. Moreover, I participate in annual gynecological screenings to stay on top of my female health. If you don't think I have already established care with a gynecologist, then you are a doctor that has a lot to learn about working with high-risk patients."

I didn't send that message back. I didn't say anything back. I just vowed never to go back. The renowned institute, specifically designed for individuals at risk for cancer, didn't know how to help me.

I showed up at my beloved OBGYN's office the next week, a blubbering mess.

"My nails are falling apart, my joints are aching, I haven't slept in three months, I am depressed, I am irritable, I am a slug, I'm so unmotivated I don't even make my kids dinner at night, I have lost ten pounds, I am anxious, I am mean, I sweat through my clothes at night, I am sad, and I am alone... I am not suicidal, but I cannot go on living like this."

"Yes, you are in menopause and your very low dose hormone therapy is not doing anything for you. You are young and your body is craving hormones. Have you ever considered bio-identical hormone therapy?"

I felt like the clouds opened up and the sunshine burst through. I didn't know anything about bio-identical hormone therapy, but at last someone was listening.

My OBGYN referred me to a local wellness clinic that practiced bio-identical hormone therapy. I ripped that stupid estrogen patch right off my hip and marched into the clinic. There I learned that bioidenticals consist of hormones that are molecularly identical to our own hormones and are derived from soy and yams. The hormones replaced are estrogen, progesterone and testosterone. I started the hormone therapy right away.

It took me several months to notice a difference in the way I felt. One afternoon I caught myself singing along to the radio in the car and it hit me that I had not done that in so long. My mood was so much brighter. I was happier, my joints didn't ache anymore, my nails grew back normally, I treated my husband nicer, I started running again, I gained 15 pounds back (which was a great thing for me as I am a happy eater), my night sweats were gone, and I was able to *sleep* again.

There is still a lot of controversy over hormone replacement therapy due to a seriously flawed and misleading study conducted by the Women's Health Institute in 2002.[xxiii] One of the lead investigators on the study, Dr. Robert Langer, has publicly criticized the study. "Good science became distorted and ultimately caused substantial and ongoing harm to women for whom appropriate and beneficial treatment was either stopped or never started," Langer wrote in the Climacteric Journal in 2017[xxiv]. The study is said to be flawed due to the many women involved in the study who had pre-existing risk factors such as heart disease and obesity. These women undoubtedly suffered consequences of the estrogen during the therapy, but not necessarily *because* of the therapy. This faulty study led providers to cease hormone therapy on approximately 80% of women.

We are still feeling the effects of the flawed study. Most

providers are untrained or unwilling to start women on hormone therapy. Bio-identical hormone therapy is even more controversial because of the lack of evidence and literature to prove its safety and efficacy. For me, the benefits of the therapy outweigh the risks. I would even go so far as to say that bio-identical hormones have served me better than my own natural hormones did.

After my oophorectomy in January 2018 and my bleeding complication, I continued to bleed. And bleed and bleed. How ironic that I was infertile with no ovaries, yet I was on the period from hell. I wore a pad every single day for 467 days. Yes, I counted.

My doctor adjusted my hormone dosage many times (a nice perk to bio-identical therapy) to try to stop the bleeding. I had a uterine ultrasound to ensure my lining wasn't too thick and even endured a uterine biopsy to make sure the tissue was healthy. Everything looked great, yet the bleeding continued. My uterus was having her last laugh. I was sure of it.

A hysterectomy typically requires eight weeks for recovery. That meant no working and no running. I didn't have that kind of time. Yes, I should have done it all in the first place. I'll probably kick myself forever for that.

While I waited for the right time in my life for my last female organ to come out, I opted for a uterine ablation instead—my ninth surgery thus far in my 36 years on this planet. The ablation of the endometrium prevents the buildup of lining, thus no bleeding. This way I could push the hysterectomy off even further.

Other people always have an opinion about the decisions we make. During one TV interview we did for a local station, the reporter challenged me on what message my decision to ablate (rather than have the total hysterectomy) would send to other women.

She argued, "There is never going to be a right time for that mammogram, that colonoscopy, that minor surgery. That's an excuse anyone can use."

This isn't an excuse, I thought.

"I did what I needed to do to save my life. I had my breasts removed when I was 22 years old. I had my ovaries ripped out of my belly button, ending my ability to ever have another baby. I did what I needed to do to eliminate my risks of cancer. The uterus poses no risk to me, other than the nuisance of bleeding. You're right, excuses I am using. Marathon training, working, taking care of my family. Sheesh, what a terrible example I am for women!"

I must clarify, again, I didn't say this, I just thought it. We are always going to be judged for the decisions we make and choose to share publicly, but no one is entitled to an opinion unless they have walked in our shoes. The BRCA mutation positive did not come with a handbook along with the results letter. It is a world I must navigate to save my life, and I am doing the best I can.

My new mantra has become, "Whatever lies ahead, let me face it with dignity and strength." Being a BRCA1 mutation carrier is not what defines me, but it is an undeniable piece of me.

I recently read a quote from St. Augustine, "I do not pray for a lighter load. I pray for stronger shoulders." This is what I always needed and what I will strive to achieve in the good, the bad, and otherwise days ahead. Give me strong shoulders on my little BRCA1 riddled body to live this incredible life.

Still I Rise
Maureen

Was my second genetic test a false negative? Or maybe the first one was a false positive? Where do I go from here? There were so many questions and yet no answers. Why did this happen? How did this happen? Was I really negative? Maybe the second test was wrong. What about the third test? Could I trust any genetic test? Did my blood get switched with someone else's in the study? Did multiple people's samples get mixed up? Or was it simply a reporting error?

I wanted to feel grateful to be negative, to not have to endure yet another life-altering surgery, to have my life back. But was I?

To move forward, I needed closure. I needed answers.

And so the journey for those answers began.

The first question I desperately needed answered was if this was a sample mix up. And, if so, did my sample get switched with my sister Kathryn's? My siblings and I all had our blood drawn on the same day, in the same doctor's office. Our initial fear was that my sample got switched with Kathryn's sample. Dr. Lynch told her she was negative. Now that I was negative, maybe she was positive.

So, Kathryn went to the genetic counselor's office to get tested through a commercial lab. And then we waited. Two long weeks. When we got the confirmation that she was, indeed, negative, Bridget and I cried.

Kathryn responded, "Were you guys really that worried?" (She doesn't have an ounce of anxiety in her little body.)

"YES!" we blurted out simultaneously. Yes, we were worried. And, yes, we were relieved.

If a sample mix up occurred, and it wasn't with Kathryn, could it have been with another member of my extended family? I needed to talk to Creighton. Unfortunately, unanswered emails turned into unanswered phone calls. The one contact I had at the university who had actually worked with my family in the 1990s retired from the university the week I contacted her.

In an eager attempt to be heard by the university, I emailed the Dean of the School of Medicine. Shortly after, I received an email from the risk management department. Risk management? Really? I felt they were viewing me as a legal threat instead of a human being. In reality, they probably were.

However, from my understanding, my legal options were almost non-existent. The medical malpractice statute of limitation in the state of Nebraska is ten years. September 2018 was ten years and three months since I was initially told my results. I was three months too late to take legal action. Fuck.

In all honesty though, I was thankful the decision to not take legal action had been determined for me. It wasn't a decision I was ready to make. My emotions were too raw. My judgment was too clouded. And, deep down, money wouldn't have made this situation better. Money would not have brought my real breasts back.

Countless emails and phone calls later and I finally made progress. The university offered to pay for another genetic test through a commercial lab. I returned to my genetic counselor to have more blood drawn. This time, my sisters joined me.

Two weeks later, the commercial lab confirmed what the other lab said: I was BRCA1 negative.

The university, however, was reluctant to confirm the current lab results. They still saw me as a legal threat. They did not feel confident the two commercial labs were using the right methodology to find the mutation. The university representative helped me understand that my family had a big mutation, and ironically, big mutations are difficult to find. Mutations come in different sizes. Our mutation was 1070bp. Typically, the methodology used by commercial labs can only reliably find mutations less than 250bp. In a nutshell, the labs may have missed my mutation.

In essence, my mutation was too big to be seen. I didn't fully understand this until a geneticist explained it to me.

When DNA is tested, it is sliced into very, very small pieces. It is then put back together. This is when they can see errors and inconsistencies in the pieces, especially small pieces. However, when large pieces of a gene are missing, there are no inconsistencies to see, because almost the entire gene is gone. This is complicated, and I am far from a geneticist to be able to explain it adequately, so just trust me. Bigger = harder to see.

So, the university ordered *another* test, this time through Myriad. Myriad is the gold standard in commercial genetic tests and the original patent holder on the BRCA gene mutation. The Supreme Court would not uphold the patent, which is why many commercial labs now exist. When Myriad lost the patent, other labs were allowed to start testing for the BRCA gene. Still today though, Myriad is the most reputable commercial lab with a 99.98% analytic sensitivity.

So, I gave my sample, and waited. This time, however, I waited six long, excruciating weeks. Initially I'd been told the results would be ready in two to three weeks. After four weeks, I was told my results had been delayed. Well, obviously. After five weeks, they explained they needed to do additional testing. The quality of my sample was poor. While it had passed the first round of testing, it didn't pass a second.

My head (and heart) went in every direction: *I must be positive, I must be negative, I must be... what am I?*

I received news the following Monday (six weeks plus) that my DNA passed both their quality standards and they had an answer. Just "two to three more days" for it to be analyzed, they said. Four excruciating days later, I got *the* call. Myriad confirmed what I both hoped and dreaded. I was, indeed, negative for the BRCA1 gene mutation.

This experience opened my eyes to the expanding world of genetic testing. These days, genetic testing has become so commonplace that individuals can test themselves in their own homes with a commercial test kit. After spitting into a cup and mailing it to a lab, curious information seekers can find out their results via email within weeks. But accurate, complex genetic testing is just not that simple. It is not black and white. It is a gray, evolving discipline.

Creighton was never able to completely explain to me why my test results were negative. Legally, they didn't have to. I later learned that the error most likely occurred because the research that Dr. Lynch conducted was a genetic linkage study. It was designed to identify the chromosomal location of defect genes or the distance between genes, not to isolate genes themselves. While his research still helped advance the study of hereditary cancers, there was a flaw to it—a flaw that altered my life.

If I said I wasn't angry, I would be lying. I was fucking pissed. How could I not be? But holding onto that anger did nothing but hurt me more. I had to let it go. I had to focus on the good. Dr. Lynch did great things. My life is filled with love from beautiful people. My future is brighter than ever.

If I have learned one thing from this, it is...well, it's not one thing at all. It's a million little things. I learned an incredible amount of information about genetics, more than I ever thought I would know. I learned that the mutation my family has is "novel" which means Myriad had never seen it before. This was mind boggling to me. I asked a geneticist at Creighton if that meant we were special, and he laughed. But that does tell us that there are a lot of variations of mutations and new ones are continuing to be discovered every day.

And that's what is so fascinating, yet incredibly frustrating, about genetics. We know a lot today. But we don't know everything. Errors occur. Deletions go undetected. Some mutations are still unknown. We need to trust genetic testing but also understand its limitations.

I've also learned to be an advocate for my health. I blindly trusted Dr. Lynch. We all did. And why not? He was the goddamn "Father of Hereditary Cancer," after all. I had no reason not to trust him, his research, and his renowned medical community. Even so, a voice inside of me warned, *What if... what if he was wrong?* So I asked him. I looked him in the eyes and asked him if he could be wrong. I advocated for myself. And he answered me in a way that communicated absolute certainty... and he was wrong. I learned to never be afraid to question something that does not feel right.

Most importantly, what I learned from having a misdiagnosed BRCA1 gene mutation, and what will hopefully help me endure all the future battles coming my way, is the quote Alisha, my college roommate, sent to me so many years ago, "You can't direct the wind, but you can adjust the sail."

In life we try so hard to direct the wind. We so desperately try to grasp for control. Control over our thoughts and emotions. Control over when, how, and the number of children we have. Control over our health and our future. What my sisters and I have learned is we have very little control in this unpredictable and sometimes scary life. Life is simply about finding happiness and spending time with those you love. Nothing more. Nothing less.

PART VIII: A MALE PERSPECTIVE

Small nipples. Big concerns.

Fortunate Son
Paul Winn, only brother

My sisters asked me to provide a chapter for this book many years ago. I found emails dating back to at least 2011 politely requesting my chapter. Deadlines, warnings, and pleadings followed these. Yet, I procrastinated. My excuses were decent (nursing school, graduate school, two babies, several cross-country career-related moves). However, one thing that prevented me from putting pen to paper was my perceived lack of relevant input on the topic of hereditary breast cancer.

When it comes to my family's story, I have often felt more like a bystander witnessing a fiery car crash than one of the car's passengers. Throughout my lifetime, I've watched my mother and sisters taking turns emerging from the charred wreckage, dusting themselves off, and carrying on with life. Meanwhile, I've been the guy standing on the sidewalk, muttering, "oh, that's messed up."

One of my earliest memories of my family's cancer story occurred on a weekday morning in the fall of 1988. I was in first grade and getting ready for school when my oldest sister, Kathryn, turned to me, and in an "I know something you don't know" tone blurted out, "Mom has cancer."

Despite being seven years old and knowing almost nothing about cancer, I confidently retorted, "No, she doesn't!"

That evening while the family ate dinner, I bluntly asked my mom if Kathryn was right. I expected a reassuring, "No, Paul, your older sister is spreading malicious medical lies again." But alas, she confirmed the news.

My parents acknowledged to us children that mom was sick but shielded us from the situation's gravity. By the time my mom's cancer was discovered, it had already spread to her axillary lymph nodes. Had it taken a few more weeks, or perhaps months, cancer would have continued to her internal organs before being diagnosed. The first stop would have likely been her liver or lungs, making it stage IV cancer. It would have been lights out after that. A stage IV cancer diagnosis is a death sentence for many people. That was even more true in 1988. So like I said, things were grave. And my mother was indescribably lucky to receive her diagnosis and start chemotherapy when she did.

Later in life, when the progressive nature and early onset of my mom's cancer became apparent to me, my initial reaction was anger that my parents were not more forthcoming about her situation's seriousness. I was allowed to carry on as a blissful, and sometimes cantankerous, kid, while they were undoubtedly crippled with fear. Being a parent myself has brought clarity. My oldest daughter is currently the approximate age I was when my mom was first diagnosed. Faced with the same situation, I, too, would desperately shield her from the unnecessary agony of knowing that one of her parents could die, at least until it was all but certain.

My sisters and I attended a relatively small Catholic elementary school, and word of the cancer diagnosis quickly spread like those metastasizing cells in my mom's body. One morning at school, the daily prayer over the intercom ended with "...and pray for Susan Winn." My teacher must have seen the look of confusion on my face because she pulled me aside and (quite poorly) tried to comfort me. She said these things were confusing, and perhaps one of my siblings had ratted the family out. I recall my thought process at the time being as follows: My mom was sick, but then she went to the doctor. She's fine now. Why are we praying for her? Is she going to die? Which of my sisters is the rat?

At home, we callously peppered my mother with questions about her breasts and the various medical brutalities to which she was being subjected. One evening at the dinner table, I point-blank asked her if I could see her mastectomy incisions. She demurred. Other times, I inquired if she would get her "breasts pumped up today," referring to the expanders that were placed before final saline implants. I was an inquisitive child.

My First Confession, also known as the Catholic Sacrament of Reconciliation, was scheduled for a weekday in the winter of 1989. My mom had undergone surgery that day, and my father was with her in the post-anesthesia care unit. Wearing my finest JCPenney dress clothes, I paced the entryway of our suburban Kansas home that evening, waiting for my parents to arrive. The phone rang periodically with brief updates. Similar to much of my mother's illness, voices were murmured and details withheld. After a few hours, I was informed that my mom couldn't shake anesthesia in time to accompany me, despite her best effort. I carry a picture of her in my mind, lying in a bed with IVs dangling from her arms, grasping for lucidity only to be pulled back into the drug-induced fog.

A family friend stepped in and brought me to the church, but I missed most of the event. They arranged for one of the priests to stay late and hear me confess my sins. In hindsight, it's amusing that Father had to put in overtime so an eight-year-old whose mom was stricken with cancer could unload his guilty conscience. Shame building begins at an early age in that institution.

My mom started chemotherapy, and her hair began falling out. Until then, cancer had been an abstract idea in my childhood brain, but it was now quite concretely personified in her newly bare scalp. Thus, the disease process became much more difficult for my parents to minimize. One afternoon, I stepped off the school bus to see my mom talking to a neighbor while wearing a brown wig. The sight made me severely uncomfortable. I begged her not to wear a wig when she came to read a book to my classroom in celebration of my half birthday. Though my mom is undoubtedly intelligent, she has long had difficulty with the pronunciation of certain words. Fittingly, I chose a book about dinosaurs for her to read to the class. She showed up and butchered "pteranodon" but wore a scarf on her head instead of the wig. The juxtaposition of my life stressors versus my mother's at that time is now so apparent.

It seemed the cancer drama went on for years, but all in all, it was probably an 18-month time span. One sunny, late Saturday afternoon, in what was perhaps the spring of 1989, I opened the door to my garage and looked outside to see my school teacher ambling up our driveway with a dour look on her face. My heart nearly stopped.

Oh no, I thought. *I've misbehaved so badly my teacher has come over on the weekend to unload on me.*

Instead, Mrs. Anderson quietly dropped off a potted plant on our front steps, didn't acknowledge me at all, and walked back to her car. These were bizarre times indeed.

With four young children, shuffling surgeries and overnight hospital stays, and living away from most of our extended family in Minnesota, my parents needed help. And help they received. My mom's 1990 book about her cancer experience, Chemo & Lunch, offers the following passage about the lady we came to know as "Grandma Dorothy:"

"The first indication that God was actually looking out for me was the arrival of Dorothy Grand at my door. I truly believe that she is an angel that God sent to help me...Dorothy heard about this poor young mother who was new to Kansas and had just been diagnosed with breast cancer. She decided to make me her mission; she wanted to be my 'Kansas City Mother.'"

My perspective of Dorothy was a bit different. Though, as I now look back to that period, my primary feeling is amusement. Without a doubt, Grandma Dorothy's selfless assistance was instrumental in righting the wayward Ship Winn. But she was also a spectacularly strange woman. We first met her in 1988, but her last clothes purchase was probably sometime around 1973. She wore navy polyester pants and paisley blouses, and in her house were piles of similar clothing stacked high on her dining table and other surfaces. My theory was that her friends kept dying, and she didn't see any reason why their wardrobes should go to waste.

Dorothy had a fervent belief in the afterlife and near-death/out-of-body experiences. She shared these stories and experiences with the four of us young children in great detail, regularly. Afternoons spent driving around in her early 1980s powder blue Plymouth Reliant were filled with stories about her late husband Eddie's death and subsequent revival. I don't remember the precise details of the story, but the gist is that Eddie died and was hovering in the corner of a hospital room for some time before eventually coming back to testify about his experiences. This was proof enough for Dorothy that God, the afterlife, and the supernatural were all real. She obsessively shared this truth with us, along with the knowledge that Eddie was probably with us right now.

Now, imagine that you either volunteer for or are tasked with the job of caring for four young children whose mom is fighting advanced cancer. What is one topic to either avoid, or at least to tread upon lightly? Death... the answer is death. So here we are... four children with their mother in the hospital, getting barraged with spooky tales of morbid demise by an old lady. Dorothy was the first person to acquaint me with the common experience of speeding through a tunnel toward a bright light as you die.

Dorothy is undoubtedly the most paranoid person I've ever met (who was not actively taking recreational drugs). One night, I awoke to the sound of John Walsh's austere voice floating into my bedroom. I quietly crept downstairs to the living room to find Dorothy asleep (or dead, I wasn't sure at the time) in a recliner with light from the television flickering across her face. She had fallen asleep watching America's Most Wanted. One of Dorothy's rules was that we could only play in our backyard in the event that if one of us gets hurt, she could gather the whole crew and rush to the hospital. To her, each of us was always in grave peril of being abducted, but she wasn't going to let it happen on her watch.

One weekend, she set up an applesauce-making operation in the kitchen and put us to work on the canning line. The concept was so peculiar that I was sure she had finally lost her mind. A few years later, the movie "Don't Tell Mom the Babysitter's Dead" came out, and I felt my experience was very similar except our weird old babysitter never died. She just told us repetitive ghost stories and used us as laborers.

I think what most irked me at the time was that she referred to herself in the third person as Grandma Dorothy and insisted we also call her Grandma Dorothy. But she wasn't my Grandma, and it pissed me off. Unsurprisingly, I misbehaved and was sometimes obstinate toward her. I was undoubtedly acting out in response to my family's stressful situation. This was before school counselors, and family therapists weren't common, so my therapy was Dorothy shooting a "Don't mess with me, I'm an octogenarian-polyester-pant-wearing-ass-kicker" look. We were all just doing our best in those days.

(After writing this last part about Dorothy, I went back and reread the chapter in my mom's book about her. It turns out my recollection is quite accurate except for one fact: she was only 66 years old at the time, hardly an octogenarian. I still can't quite believe this because, in my eyes, she was older than dirt. Other details ring true. My mom wrote in great detail about Dorothy's stories of Eddie's death, revival, testimony, and subsequent redeath. Dorothy's last name was Grand, and when not referring to herself as Grandma Dorothy, she would call herself "General Grant." Instead of the ass-kicker you want, life often gives you the one you need.)

Like my sisters, I have a pretty good recollection of blood being drawn from my arm as part of Dr. Lynch's research on familial breast cancer. I don't recall this being a painful or scary experience. Rather, it was fascinating and made me feel like a unique child. The volume of blood that they removed seemed concerning, however. As an elementary-aged child, I wondered why they needed several bags of my blood to see if there was just one strange gene.

Mom made a full recovery, and life normalized tremendously for the whole family. She penned her book, which I'm sure was a cathartic experience. I was able to continue my privileged upper-middle-class existence. But the breast cancer stuff was now tattooed into my memories. And embedded into my

DNA, as it turns out.

But first, let's talk about breasts. I've got two of them. And so do you. Recently, I had to convince my eight-year-old daughter that I, too, have breasts. She looked at me with skepticism as I told her all about male breast tissue and male breast cancer. She gave me a similarly perplexing look when I challenged her about why young girls needed to wear tops to their bathing suits before developing breasts. I admitted to her that I also didn't have a great answer to that question.

As men, we are taught to think of our breasts as either non-existent or with different terminologies, such as pectorals. It's embarrassing to have man boobs, and as a teenager, I cranked out dozens of pushups at the slightest hint that the adipose tissue on my chest was increasing in size.

My progression from adolescence to teenage years meant that breasts were less a source of familial morbidity and more the object of sexual desire. However, I couldn't undo the way I had learned to talk about breasts as a child. A girlfriend once noted how formal I sounded when referring to her breasts. "Most guys just say 'boobs,'" she told me.

Aside from my mother's triumph over breast cancer and the yet undisclosed genetic results hanging over my head, breasts continued to play a role in my adolescent and teenage years. My mom had been a long-time registered nurse in the newborn intensive care unit and decided to become a certified lactation consultant. Along with a fellow nursing coworker, she started a company, Baby's First Choice, which provided lactation consultant services to hospitals and individuals. This involved helping women who had difficulties breastfeeding and supplying women with breast pumps. For several years a lot of breastfeeding paraphernalia laid around the house. It was not uncommon to walk into the kitchen and hear my mom troubleshooting breastfeeding difficulties with a new mother on the phone. My sisters and I got used to tossing a BFC breast pump aside when climbing into the minivan. These breast pumps, enclosed in blue rigid plastic boxes approximately the size of a toolbox, were often stored in the garage.

One morning as a sophomore in high school, I was running late as usual, and while backing out of the garage in my red '93 Pontiac Grand Prix, a terrifying noise came from beneath the car. The sounds of squealing, scratching, and popping prompted me to slam the brakes, jump out, and inspect. Firmly wedged under the front bumper was a blue breast pump. And it wouldn't budge. I laid on my back and kicked it to no avail. I finally resorted to backing down the driveway before the cracked and mangled pump emerged from my car. The event caused me to be late for school. I had the impulsive urge to blurt out to the classroom that my tardiness was due to a mishap with a breast pump. Sadly, my youthful insecurity prevailed, and I sheepishly slunk into my desk 15 minutes late. As it turns out, crushing that breast pump was the only contact I had with anything related to the female breast during my high school years.

I did not spend much time ruminating about the possibility of being a BRCA1 gene carrier as a teenager and into my early 20s. To me, being a carrier was a nebulous concept that only hovered distantly in the background. But by the time I was 23 years old, the idea of me having the BRCA1 gene mutation became more like a toilet that wouldn't stop running; I'd eventually have to lift the lid of the tank and see what the hell was going on. I hoped I didn't have to call a plumber.

My impetus for finding out my BRCA1 test results was the relationship with my then-girlfriend and now wife, Amanda. We had been dating for about two years at the time. I was smitten with her kindness, intelligence, and aptitude. Our courtship was easy, natural, and fun. Getting engaged would be fun. Getting married would add even more fun to the fun! First, though, I felt she needed to know whether I was a gene carrier and that our potential children also had a 50% chance of being carriers. This was not something she asked for or even cared too much about. Our future children were very hypothetical at that time —a twinkle in my eye, as they say. But the toilet was running...

time to lift that tank lid.

On a chilly and overcast weekday morning in early 2004, I sat in a genetic counselor's office in suburban south Kansas City. My mom had accompanied me to learn the result of the test that had been performed what seemed like a lifetime ago. The blood had been drawn when I was eight, so 65% of my life had passed while those test results collected dust in Nebraska.

My mother and the counselor, a chipper middle-aged woman, chatted as I nervously shifted in my chair. The conversation moved towards the theoretical implications of me being a carrier. For a moment, I feared I had been not paying attention during the result disclosure, and we had already moved on to the next steps. The counselor could sense my irritability and asked if I was ready to hear my results.

"That's why I'm here," I curtly responded.

She opened a manila folder and slid it towards me. Positive for BRCA1.

Of course, I was positive. I never doubted that. My uneducated guess was based on Kathryn and Bridget, who had already received their results: Kathryn was negative and had light brown hair, but Bridget was positive and had dark brown hair. Since I had dark brown hair like Bridget, I would be positive too because we shared more genes. My scientifically ignorant theory had been right. Even more so, I didn't feel lucky enough to be BRCA1 negative. My luck in life had been used up on two events: being born a white man in the United States and the time in third grade when I won a Reebok bathrobe in the school carnival raffle. I was a confirmed BRCA1 carrier. Time to call the plumber.

Carrying my results, I walked to my car, where I called Amanda and told her the news. She was supportive, and we agreed to deal with future challenges as they arise. To me, receiving the positive BRCA1 result was like being told that I might someday be in a car accident; I'd continue wearing my seatbelt and try not to drive like an idiot.

In the ten years that followed, I did not pursue any proactive screening measures. This was mostly because I viewed BRCA1 as primarily a risk to my future (still hypothetical at the time) daughters.

Blessed by a Curse
Paul Winn, only brother

In my mid-20s, I left an unfulfilling career in advertising and went to nursing school at the University of Washington in Seattle. In 2013, at age 32, I received my Master's degree as an Acute Care Nurse Practitioner and began working in cardiology. Becoming a health care provider made it more difficult to ignore the sleeping beast within me that was BRCA1. I am fortunate to have received my health and science education. It significantly improved my understanding of how having BRCA1 and BRCA2 increase an individual's risk of developing cancer and how cancer affects the body. Here are some of my insights:

1. Everyone has BRCA1 and BRCA2 genes. A critical function of these genes is to repair damaged DNA in cells.

2. DNA damage is a routine and natural occurrence in the body, but it increases with frequency as we age. Certain environmental factors can accelerate DNA damage. For example, formaldehyde exposure has been shown to increase DNA damage. So do ultraviolet rays from the sun. Both formaldehyde and excess UV exposure have, therefore, been associated with increased cancer risk.

3. When a cell senses that DNA damage has occurred, it recruits the BRCA gene to produce proteins to either help repair the damaged DNA or to encourage apoptosis (cell death).

4. People who are unlucky enough to have inherited a BRCA gene mutation (i.e., a BRCA gene that doesn't function properly) have a higher likelihood that damaged DNA will not be adequately repaired.

5. One possible consequence of unrepaired DNA is a cell that reproduces rapidly and uncontrollably. This unchecked growth can become a tumor, a.k.a. malignancy, a.k.a. cancer.

6. A cancerous tumor takes up space in the body and can limit the function of the organ from which it arises. Metastasis of a tumor is when abnormal cells from one kind of tissue (for example, the lungs) spread to other parts of the body.

7. Metastatic cancer ultimately kills a person by preventing major organs from performing their job. For example, cancer that spreads to the liver will prevent it from filtering blood and producing chemicals that help digest food. The malfunction of one organ often quickly affects the function of other organs. This sets off a cascade of accelerating and destructive processes in the body. Infection, bleeding, blood clots, or respiratory failure often act as the final insult.

Men without the BRCA1 or BRCA2 gene mutation (sometimes referred to as BRCA1/2) have an approximate lifetime risk of developing breast cancer of just 0.1%, meaning that about 1 of every 1000 men from the general public will develop breast cancer. For those with BRCA1 (such as myself), the risk increases 10-fold to about 1%. For men with the BRCA2 mutation, the risk is 7-8%. All in all, these numbers are not concerning to me. But along with a higher risk of breast and ovarian cancer, BRCA1/2 mutations have shown to also create prostate cancer, pancreatic cancer, and melanoma.

I stood on a tranquil Oregon Coast beach one early morning in September 2017 and watched my two-year-old daughter, Bridget (named affectionately after my sister), squish handfuls of wet sand between her chubby fingers. Amanda and I were giving our kids one last moment at the beach before cutting our vacation short to zip back home to Portland. Bridget had been awakening each morning for the past week with successively more swollen eyelids. The evening prior, we noticed she had been stumbling and falling more frequently, probably due to the subtle, yet increasing swelling in her feet. As we drove back, a cursory internet search led me to believe that her swelling was likely due to nephrotic syndrome.

Lab testing that afternoon in the Children's ER confirmed the diagnosis. My poor child had almost undetectable levels of albumin (a kind of protein) in her blood because her kidney had stopped filtering blood properly. Within a few hours, we had already been visited by a pediatric nephrologist, and a course of treatment was planned. The next few years would entail different immunosuppressive regimens, recurrent hospital admissions for fluid removal, and ultimately achieving a permanent (at least up until now) remission from the disease.

Bridget's illness is relatively rare (about 2 in 100,000 children are diagnosed annually), and it prompted me and several of my family members to ask: could her nephrotic syndrome (an autoimmune disease) be related to BRCA1? The short answer is, probably not. But the question led me to seek out a genetics counselor. It had been about 13 years since I had received my gene carrier results. I was curious if there was a possible genetic link to my child's illness. I also wanted to know if there were any new cancer screening guidelines for men with the BRCA1 gene mutation.

The geneticist was friendly but had a mostly businesslike demeanor. Her bold, red hair and thick Irish accent made me wonder how the hell she ended up in Oregon. The dimly lamp-lit, basement office where she saw patients included multiple seating options where you could receive bad news. She took a detailed history but was befuddled when I could not provide any paperwork that proved I was positive for BRCA1.

"How do you know you are positive if you don't have any documentation?" she asked.

"I lost the paperwork, but my family was part of a big research study by Dr. Henry Lynch," I told her, as if to say, "just Google me."

We ultimately decided that I should get retested for BRCA1. And once again, I tested positive. Exactly one year later, Maureen called me sobbing with the baffling news that she was not, as we previously thought, BRCA positive. However, my relatively recent confirmatory results prevented me from having any optimism that there was also a laboratory error in my favor.

A follow-up appointment with my geneticist involved discussing further surveillance measures for myself and possibly my children. In 2017, there were no established guidelines for what types of cancer screening should be performed on men who have the BRCA1/2 mutation. The research shows that with

BRCA1, my lifetime risk of developing pancreatic cancer is about four to six times higher than the general population. My chance of developing prostate cancer is about fourteen times higher than the average man. These are not numbers to be taken lightly.

Pancreatic cancer, in particular, scares me because most cases are not discovered until they are advanced. I worked as a gastroenterology nurse practitioner for three years, caring for numerous patients with pancreatic cancer. Many of them were experiencing problems from liver metastasis or a tumor that was blocking the GI tract. The overall prognosis for pancreatic cancer is poor, with a five-year-survival rate of about 9%. Watching these patients decline has taught me that death, cancer death, in particular, is many things but dignified.

Knowledge is power, but it can also be anxiety-provoking. I asked my geneticist for a referral to a gastroenterologist, a pancreatic specialist, in particular, to discuss pancreatic cancer screening recommendations. The doctor I ended up seeing happened to be a colleague with whom I had interacted in the hospital on a semi-regular basis. He kindly listened to my concerns and then performed the routine auscultating, tapping, and palpating of my abdomen.

After his physical exam, the well-respected, Iraqi-born physician said, "so tell me... do you ever have abdominal pain?"

"I mean, not regularly," I responded.

"Yes, of course," he said knowingly, "but have you EVER had abdominal pain?"

I picked up what he was saying, albeit a second late. "Oh yeah, I've had abdominal pain," I assured him.

"CT scan abdomen," he said decisively.

"Okay, how often do you want me to be screened?" I asked. "That's it. If it's negative, no cancer." he replied sharply, trying to wrap up our appointment.

"Yeah, but doesn't my risk of pancreatic cancer increase as I age?" I questioned, sitting on the exam table.

He turned to leave the room. "Look, this is how I run my

practice," he said. "There are no guidelines, so insurance isn't going to pay for testing. Goodbye."

It wasn't the first conversation I'd attempted to have with a doctor while they actively walked away. As a nurse, I had been hung up on by physicians while I was mid-sentence, asking a question. As a male nurse practitioner, this was more seldom but still happened.

I never scheduled the CT scan. Paying a bunch of money to have my abdomen bombarded with radiation when I was pretty damn sure I didn't have pancreatic cancer at that moment didn't seem prudent.

In hindsight, I hoped that a discussion with the gastro-enterologist would produce a mutually agreed upon follow-up plan that we both knew was likely to change as knowledge evolved. Instead, I felt dismissed. I suspect that not knowing how to act on a positive result will be an ongoing theme as genetic testing becomes more commonplace. Both health care providers and patients will share the frustration of being unsure of how to proceed. As a cancer gene carrier and provider, I am in a unique position to know how it feels on both sides of the conversation

Over the past few years, headway has been made regarding screening recommendations for men with BRCA1/2. The Basser Center for BRCA at Penn Medicine has developed recommendations specifically for men with BRCA1/2. These include yearly clinical breast exams starting at age 35 and prostate cancer screening starting at age 40 for BRCA2 carriers. However, pancreatic cancer screening guidelines are still not included in recommendations. In August of 2019, the U.S. Preventative Service Task Force (USPSTF) updated their screening recommendations for women with BRCA1/2 but did not include BRCA1/2 positive men's recommendations. This was criticized as a missed opportunity, particularly regarding prostate cancer screening, because 6% of men with metastatic prostate cancer are found to be BRCA1/2 carriers.

There's a saying among some recovering alcoholics—that

they are not just grateful to be sober, but even more grateful to be an alcoholic. Having gratitude for being cursed by a disease seems like a paradox. Yet, I have similar feelings about being a BRCA1 gene mutation carrier. I am blessed, because like the recovering alcoholic, I am aware of my affliction, and I have used that awareness to improve my life.

I am fortunate to have access to so many cancer treatment options that were not available to my maternal grandmother, Elda, who died at age 44, leaving five children behind. I am fortunate to know about inheritable gene mutations and early screening; information not available to my mother, Susan, who was broadsided by breast cancer at age 32. As a man, I am fortunate that my breast cancer risk is in the single digits, as compared to my sisters, Bridget and Maureen, who went under the knife to mitigate their all but guaranteed cancer diagnosis.

To return to my fiery-car-crash-bystander analogy, I am fortunate to have been a witness to the suffering experienced by Elda, Susan, Bridget, Maureen, and many other women in my extended family. Their hardship and agony were real, but not in vain, because they inspired awareness within the family and discovery within the scientific community. This awareness and discovery will undoubtedly save many BRCA1/2 gene mutation carriers from an early, preventable death.

As I type this, my two young daughters peacefully slumber in their beds. They are unaware that inside the nucleus of each cell in their body, on the long arm of chromosome number 17, in position 17q21, lies the BRCA1 gene. They don't know that there are 81,000 pairs of DNA contained within 24 exons on the BRCA1 gene. At some point in the next few years, their blood will be collected and a close look at exon number 16 might reveal an incredibly small amount of missing genetic material, also known as a deletion. If that is the case, I have inadvertently passed them BRCA1 gene mutation.

If either of my daughters should learn they have inherited the gene mutation, I know they will find overwhelming support from my sisters, mother, and the rest of our family. But regardless of their test results, I hope that Norah and Bridget will find strength from this book and be inspired by the courage, perseverance, and humility the women in my family have shown. I hope this book teaches them that humor and vulgarity are completely appropriate responses to life's bullshit. Lastly, I hope they will feel as oddly fortunate as I do to be blessed by a curse.

NOTE FROM
AUTHORS

Note from Authors

If you get nothing else from this book, it is the importance of being an advocate for your own health. No one can do it better than you. If we can offer one last bit of advice, it is this:

Listen to that voice inside your head.

Trust your doctor, but also trust your intuition.

Don't be intimidated when a doctor tells you your intuition is wrong.

You are power.

You know your body better than anyone.

Doctors can be wrong, and so can tests.

Don't stop seeking answers and opinions until you are satisfied.

If for any reason, whether rational or not, you do not feel confident with your genetic test results, do not hesitate to get retested.

And, lastly, love your family dearly and hold them close. Life is fragile and harder than we deserve. Loved ones make the journey a little easier and a lot more beautiful.

Sincerely,
Kathryn, Paul, Bridget & Maureen

REFERENCES

References

1. "A Conversation with Mary-Claire King" Neill, U., (updated in 2019). *The Journal of Clinical Investigation*, 129(1):1–3. https://doi.org/10.1172/JCI126050.

2. "About Genetic Testing," Myriad Genetics, accessed on June 11,2019,https://myriad.com/healthcare-professionals/about-genetic-testing/overview/

3. American Cancer Society (2014.) Early Theories About Cancer Causes. Retrieved June 2020 from www.cancer.org/cancer/cancer-basics

4. "ASCO Remembers Cancer Genetics Pioneer Dr. Henry T. Lynch," American Society of Clinical Oncology (ASCO), accessed 2020, https://connection.asco.org/magazine/society-member-news/asco-remembers-cancer-genetics-pioneer-dr-henry-t-lynch

5. "A Tribute to Dr. Henry T. Lynch," Lynch Syndrome International (LSI), Archived from the original on December 2, 2013,https://web.archive.org/web/20131203004247/http://www.lynchcancers.com/index.php/tribute-to-dr.-henry-t.-lynch

6. "Advice, like youth, probably just wasted on the young," Chicago Tribune, Mary Schmich, June 1, 1997, https://www.chicagotribune.com/columns/chi-schmich-sunscreen-column-column.html?q=wear+sunscreen "Bell's Palsy," Mayo Clinic, accessed in 2020, https://www.mayoclinic.org/diseases-conditions/bells-palsy/symptoms-causes/syc-20370028

7. "Best serum biomarker combination for ovarian cancer classification," US National Library of Medicine National Institutes of Health, accessed on December 11th, 2019, https://www.ncbi.nlm.nih.gov/pmc/articles/PMC6219009/

#:~:text=One%20of%20the%20most%20popular,many %20women%20with%20ovarian%20cancer

8. "Breast Reconstruction," BreastCancer.org, accessed on February 12, 2019, https://www.breastcancer.org/treatment/surgery/reconstruction

9. Bourne, Edmond. Anxiety and Phobia Workbook, 2011.

10. "CA125 in Ovarian Cancer," US National Library of Medicine National Institutes of Health, accessed on April 4th, 2018, https://www.ncbi.nlm.nih.gov/pmc/articles/PMC2872496/

11. *Chemo and Lunch: One Woman's Victory over Hereditary Breast Cancer*, Susan Winn, 1990

12. "Everything You Should Know About Flat Warts," Healthline, updated March 12, 2020, https://www.healthline.com/health/skin-disorders/flat-warts#prevention

13. "Genetic Linkage Analysis," Basic Science Seminars on Neurology, accessed on January 19, 2020, https://jamanetwork.com/journals/jamaneurology/fullarticle/775035

14. "Henry T. Lynch." Creighton University, accessed 2020, http://medschool.creighton.edu/centers/hcc/history/henrytlynch/

15. "How Long Do Implants last?" Healthline, Accessed on June 24, 2020, https://www.healthline.com/health/how-long-do-implants-last

16. "Infertility: Beta 3 Integrin," The Bump, accessed in 2020, https://forums.thebump.com/discussion/12131368/beta-integrin-3-test

17. "Infertility, " Fertility Factor, accessed on May 20, 2020, https://fertilityfactor.com/

18. Langer, R.D. (2017) The evidence base for HRT: what can we believe? Climacteric, 20:2, 91-96, DOI: 10.1080/13697137.2017.1280251

19. Mauvais-Jarvis F., Clegg D..J, and Hevener A.L. (2013). The role of estrogens in control of energy balance and glucose homeostasis. *Endocrine Reviews.* 34(3), 309–338. doi:10.1210/er.2012-1055

20. "Myriad Genetics: In the eye of the policy storm," US National Library of Medicine National Institutes of Health, accessed on April 9th, 2019, https://www.ncbi.nlm.nih.gov/pmc/articles/PMC3037261/

21. "Preimplantation Genetic Testing," American Society for Reproductive Medicine, last modified May 1st, 2014. https://americanpregnancy.org/getting-pregnant/preimplantation-genetic-diagnosis

22. Scholler, N., & Urban, N. (2007). CA125 in Ovarian Cancer. Biomarkers in medicine, 1(4),513–523. doi:10.2217/17520363.1.4.5

23. "The World's First-Test Tube Baby," ThoughtCo, Accessed February 11, 2020, https://www.thoughtco.com/first-test-tube-baby-louise-brown-1779783

24. "Why Breast Reconstruction Is Not A Boob Job!," Nancy's Point, accessed on May 17, 2020, https://nancyspoint.com/why-reconstruction-is-not-a-boob-job/

25. Wikipedia contributors. (2020, June 22). BRCA1. In Wikipedia, The Free Encyclopedia. Retrieved 23:27, June 24, 2020,

from   https://en.wikipedia.org/w/index.php?
title=BRCA1&oldid=963868423

Endnotes

[i] *Chemo and Lunch: One Woman's Victory over Hereditary Breast Cancer,*
Susan Winn, 1990

[ii] "What Celebrities Have or Have Had Breast Cancer?" National
Breast Cancer Foundation, Inc, accessed on June 25, 2020, https://
www.nationalbreastcancer.org/about-breast-cancer/celebrities

[iii] "ASCO Remembers Cancer Genetics Pioneer Dr. Henry T.
Lynch," American Society of Clinical Oncology (ASCO), accessed
2020, https://connection.asco.org/magazine/society-member-news/
asco-remembers-cancer-genetics-pioneer-dr-henry-t-lynch

[iv] American Cancer Society (2014.) Early Theories About Cancer
Causes. Retrieved June 2020 from www.cancer.org/cancer/cancer-
basics

[v] American Cancer Society (2014.) Early Theories About Cancer Causes.
Retrieved June 2020 from www.cancer.org/cancer/cancer-basics

[vi] "A Tribute to Dr. Henry T. Lynch," Lynch Syndrome International
(LSI), Archived from the original on
December 2, 2013, https://web.archive.org/web/20131203004247/
http://www.lynchcancers.com/index.php/tribute-to-dr.-henry-t.-
lynch

[vii] "Henry T. Lynch." Creighton University, accessed 2020,
http://medschool.creighton.edu/centers/hcc/history/henrytlynch/

[viii] "Henry T. Lynch." Creighton University, accessed 2020,
http://medschool.creighton.edu/centers/hcc/history/henrytlynch/

[ix] "Henry T. Lynch." Creighton University, accessed 2020,

http://medschool.creighton.edu/centers/hcc/history/henrytlynch/

[x] "A Conversation with Mary-Claire King" Ncill, U., (updated in 2019). *The Journal of Clinical Investigation*, 129(1):1–3. https://doi.org/10.1172/JCI126050.

[xi] "Everything You Should Know About Flat Warts," Healthline, updated March 12, 2020, https://www.healthline.com/health/skin-disorders/flat-warts#prevention

[xii] "The World's First-Test Tube Baby," ThoughtCo, Accessed February 11, 2020, https://www.thoughtco.com/first-test-tube-baby-louise-brown-1779783

[xiii] "Infertility," Fertility Factor, accessed on May 20, 2020, https://fertilityfactor.com/

[xiv] "Preimplantation Genetic Testing," American Society for Reproductive Medicine, last modified May 1st, 2014. https://americanpregnancy.org/getting-pregnant/preimplantation-genetic-diagnosis

[xv] Breastcancer.org/nipple-sparing
[xvi]
"How Long Do Implants last?" Healthline, Accessed on June 24, 2020, https://www.healthline.com/health/how-long-do-implants-last

[xvii] "Breast Reconstruction," BreastCancer.org, accessed on February 12, 2019, https://www.breastcancer.org/treatment/surgery/reconstruction

[xviii] "Direct-to-implant breast reconstruction," Amy S. Colwell, AME Publishing Company, November 2012, https://www.ncbi.nlm.nih.gov/pmc/articles/PMC4115696/

[xix] "Infertility: Beta 3 Integrin," The Bump, accessed in 2020, https://forums.thebump.com/discussion/12131368/beta-integrin-3-test

[xx]"Advice, like youth, probably just wasted on

the young," Chicago Tribune, Mary Schmich, June 1, 1997, https://www.chicagotribune.com/columns/chi-schmich-sunscreen-column-column.html?q=wear+sunscreen

[xxi] Mauvais-Jarvis F., Clegg D.J., and Hevener A.L. (2013). The role of estrogens in control of energy balance and glucose homeostasis. *Endocrine Reviews*. 34(3), 309–338. doi:10.1210/er.2012-1055

[xxii] "Bell's Palsy," Mayo Clinic, accessed in 2020, https://www.mayoclinic.org/diseases-conditions/bells-palsy/symptoms-causes/syc-20370028

[xxiii] Langer, R.D. (2017) The evidence base for HRT: what can we believe? *Climacteric*, 20:2, 91-96, DOI: 10.1080/13697137.2017.1280251

[xxiv] Langer, R.D. (2017) The evidence base for HRT: what can we believe? *Climacteric*, 20:2, 91-96, DOI: 10.1080/13697137.2017.1280251

Made in the USA
Monee, IL
17 June 2021